MW00715027

PRACTICAL RELIGION

by

Catherine Booth

Salvation Books
The Salvation Army International Headquarters
London, United Kingdom

First published as a collection in 1878
Revised edition 2008

Copyright © 2008
The General of The Salvation Army

ISBN 978-0-85412-772-6

Cover design by Nathan Sigauke

Published by Salvation Books
The Salvation Army International Headquarters
101 Queen Victoria Street, London EC4V 4EH
United Kingdom

Printed by UK Territory Print & Design Unit

CONTENTS

SERIES INTRODUCTION
'CLASSIC SALVATIONIST TEXTS'

This series is intended to help a new generation of readers become familiar with works published across the years by The Salvation Army and which over time have come to be regarded as 'classics' in Salvationist circles and even beyond.

It is hoped also that these republications might lead to a rediscovery of them and the truths they convey by those who once read them. They live on not only for their content, but also for the passionate spirit that breathes through what is written.

Salvationists have no desire to live in the past, but we are ready to recognise the debt we owe to those who have gone before. We look to the future, under God, taking with us the sacred heritage he has given. These writings are part of that heritage.

I hope and pray that this series will help and inspire all who use it, and that some will be prompted to contribute in written form to modern Salvationist literature in an age that needs also the old, eternal truths expressed in language for the 21st century.

The series is dedicated to the glory of God.

Shaw Clifton
General
London, July 2007

PREFACE

It will be observed that these papers are mostly the reports of addresses delivered at various times, in various places where God has called me to witness for him. I have frequently been asked to publish them in one volume by those who have listened to me with thankfulness to God and profit to themselves. Compelled in great measure to desist for a season from public speaking by bodily infirmity, I seize the opportunity to repeat on paper what I have been privileged to express in (to me) brighter days. I pray that I may thus be allowed to continue my testimony against the attempt, now so prevalent, to serve both God and mammon, and to warn and teach everyone to flee from the wrath to come by avoiding every sin and the very appearance of evil, and by devoting themselves without reserve to the service of God and the salvation of the world: and I trust that he who has given to me these thoughts and words may restore to me the power to speak again, and to speak more boldly still. Thank God, brighter days have come than I have ever known before, God having set before me an open door to vast multitudes all over the world who, three years ago, were not within our reach. In *Aggressive Christianity* and *Godliness* may be found some of my later addresses to these millions. But our views have no way changed, and I am thankful to find increasing need to supply the demand for the old volume.

Catherine Booth
London, December 1878

One

The training of children – an address to parents

My dear friends, I feel a special interest in addressing you on the present occasion; a sort of family feeling resulting from a community of interests which is always inspiring. I have sometimes thought, when I have heard men talking to women on their duties as wives and mothers, their trials and difficulties, and so on, 'Ah, it is all very good, but you don't know much about it, after all.' Now, I do not come to speak to you tonight under this disadvantage, at any rate. I do know something of the things of which I speak. Having had a large and young family, I have had some experience of the anxiety, toil and difficulty required in the training and management of young children. It is because I am so well acquainted with the weight of the trials and duties of maternity that I sympathise so deeply with mothers, and would fain help to lighten their burdens by a little practical advice and instruction.

I presume that all here are agreed as to the responsibility devolving on parents to give some sort of training to their children. There is not a mother here who would think it right to leave her child to grow up without discipline or training of some kind! Then the question for us to consider is, 'What sort of training does God, and our duty to our children, require from us?'

In order to get at the answer to this question, the first important matter for a parent to settle in her own mind, is this: 'To whom does this child belong?' Is it mine, or is it the Lord's? Surely, this question should not need any discussion, at least by Christian parents! For do we not recognise, even before they are born, that they are peculiarly and exclusively a heritage from the Lord; and when they came into the world, the first effort we put forth was to hold them up and offer them to him? And again, in their christening we acknowledged that they belonged to him, and promised to train them for his glory.

Now the keeping of this one fact before the mind of a mother will be the best guiding principle in training; and it is because Christian parents so often forget whose their children are that they make such mistakes in training them. I say, then, to you mothers here, settle it in your minds that your child belongs absolutely to God, and not to you. You are only stewards for God, holding your children to nurse them and train them for him.

This responsibility arises first out of the command and ordination of God. Both under the old and new dispensations, the Lord has, in the most emphatic and solemn manner, laid the obligation on parents to train their children for him; he commands it, to whom both parents and children exclusively belong.

Secondly, this responsibility arises out of the nature of the relationship between parent and child. The parent is in the most complete sense the owner, the guardian, the director, and controller of the child. Its utter helplessness and ignorance when it first comes into the world throws it completely under the power of, and at the discretion of, its parents. The poor little infant has no choice but to be led as its parents lead it; no option but to be directed, trained, and developed physically, mentally, and spiritually as its parents develop it; and it is during these early stages of helplessness and ignorance that the impetus is generally given to its future life.

There is an old adage, 'They who rock the cradle rule the world', and they certainly do; but I am afraid that the world has been very badly ruled, just because those who rock the cradle have not known how to train the child. Napoleon once said that 'the great want of France was mothers'; and I am afraid we may say to a greater extent than ever before in our history that the great want of England is mothers: right-minded, able, competent, Christian mothers, who realise their responsibility to God and to their children, and who are resolved at all costs and sacrifices to discharge it.

Thirdly, this responsibility arises out of our ability for the task. We are able to train our children in the way they should go, or God would not have enjoined it upon us. He required every father and mother in Israel to train their children for him. He admitted of no exception, no excuse; and in the New Testament it is assumed as a first duty with believers to train up their children 'in the nurture and admonition of the Lord'. The training God requires is a moral training: the inspiring of the child with the love of goodness, truth and righteousness, and leading him to its practice and exercise in all the duties and emergencies of life.

Now, any parent, however poor, unlearned, or occupied, can do this if only she has the grace of God in her heart, and will take the trouble. Training a child in the way he should go does not necessarily imply a scholastic training. All parents have not the power to educate their children, nor to do much for them temporally. They cannot put them in a position to get much of this world's goods. But these things are not included in right training. A child may be trained for the highest moral and spiritual development without these; and, where there is natural ability, for the highest mental development also.

This is abundantly established in the histories of some of our great men. We know what kind of homes some of them were trained in, what humble parentage some of them had, what little learning they had in their early days; but, nevertheless, they were trained in the way they should go, and having been set going in the right path, when they came to mature years they did not fail to help themselves. No poor parent need be discouraged because he cannot educate his children in the popular sense.

God does not require of us more than we can do, and if we train our children, as far as is possible to us, in the way they should go, they will then go in that way for themselves. God's providence and spirit and their own bias will guide them on and on, as it has done many a son of poor parents, to prosperity, usefulness and honour in this world, as well as to eternal glory in the next.

But, fourthly, this responsibility is increased by the opportunity which parents possess, and especially mothers, to train their children. Being thrown constantly with them, having them continually under our eye by night and by day, when no one else is there, being acquainted with all their peculiarities of disposition, and entering into all their joys and sorrows, what splendid opportunities occur daily for pruning, correcting, inspiring, leading and encouraging them, as the case may require.

Then, fifthly, what an awful responsibility arises out of the influence which God has given us over our children. This influence is irresistible until parents by their own injudicious conduct fritter it away. A little child who has been rightly trained has unbounded, unquestioning confidence in its parents; what father or mother says is, to it, an end of all controversy; it never seeks for further proof.

This influence wisely used will never wear out, but will spread like an atmosphere around the child's moral nature, moulding and fashioning all his future life. I sometimes meet with parents who tell me that at the age of 16 or 17, their children have become quite unmanageable, and that they have lost all their influence over them. I cannot tell you which I pity most – such children, or such parents.

One of the worst signs of our times is the little respect which children seem to have for their parents. There are numbers of boys and girls of from 12 to 17 years of age over whom their parents have little or no control. But how has this come to pass? Did these children leap all at once from the restraints and barriers of parental affection and authority? Oh no, it has been the result of the imperceptible growth of years of insubordination and want of proper discipline; the gradual loss of parental influence until they have thrown it off altogether, and resolved to do as they please. Hence the terrible exhibitions we have of youthful depravity, lawlessness and rebellion.

Well, I think I hear some mother say: 'I see, I feel my responsibility, and I long to train my children in the way they should go, but how am I to do it?'

First let as look at the meaning of the word 'train'.

It does not mean merely to teach. Some parents seem to have the notion that all they have to do in training their children aright is to teach them. So they cram them with religious sentiment and truth, making them commit to memory the catechism, large portions of Scripture, a great many hymns and so on. All very good as far as it goes, but which may all be done without a single stroke of real training such as God requires, and such as the hearts of our children need.

Nay, this mere teaching, informing the head without interesting or influencing the heart, frequently drives children off from God and goodness, and makes them hate, instead of love, everything connected with religion.

In the early part of my married life, when my dear husband was travelling very much from place to place, I was frequently thrown into the houses of leading families in churches for three or four weeks at a time, and I used to say to myself, 'How is it that these children seem frequently to have a more inveterate dislike for religion and religious things, than the children of worldly people who make no profession?'

Subsequent observations and experience have shown me the reason. It is because such parents inform the head without training the heart. They teach what they neither practise themselves nor take the trouble to see that their children practise, and the children see through the hollow sham and learn to despise both their parents and their religion.

Mother, if you want to train your child you must practise what you teach, and you must show him how to practise it also, and you must, at all costs of trouble and care, see that he does it.

Suppose, by way of illustration, that you have a vine, and that this vine is endowed with reason and will and moral sense. You say to your vine-dresser: 'Now, I want that vine trained; made to grow in a particular way so that it may bear the largest amount of fruit possible to it.'

Suppose your vinedresser goes to your vine every morning and says to it, 'Now, you must let that branch grow in this direction, and that branch grow in another; you are not to put forth too many shoots here, nor too many tendrils there; you must not waste your sap in too many leaves.' And having told it what to do and how to grow, he shuts it up and leaves it to itself.

This is precisely the way many good people act towards their children. But lo! the vine grows as it likes; nature is too strong for mere theory; words will not curb its exuberance, nor check its waywardness. Your vinedresser must do something more effectual than talking. He must nail that branch where he wishes it to grow; he must cut away what he sees to be superfluous; he must lop, and prune and dress it, if it is to be trained for beauty and for fruitfulness. And just so, mother, if you want your child to be trained for God and righteousness you must prune, and curb and propel and lead it in the way in which it should go.

But some mother says: 'What a deal of trouble!' Ah, that is just why many parents fail; they are afraid of trouble; but, as Mrs Stowe says, 'If you will not take the trouble to train Charlie when he is a little boy, he will give you a great deal more trouble when he is a big one.' Many a foolish mother, to spare herself trouble, has left her children to themselves, and 'a child left to himself bringeth his mother to shame!'

Many parents teach their children in theory the right way, but by their negligence and indifference train them in just the opposite. See that mother seated at some important piece of work which she is anxious to finish. Her three little children are playing around her – one with his picture book, another with his horse and cart, and baby with her doll. It is Monday afternoon, and only yesterday she was giving those children a lesson on the importance of love and goodwill amongst themselves; that was the teaching, now comes the training.

Presently Charlie gets tired of his pictures, and, without asking permission, takes the horse and cart from his younger brother, whereupon there is a scream, and presently a fight. Instead of laying aside her work, restoring the rightful property, explaining to Charlie that it is unjust and unkind to take his brother's toys, and to the younger one that he should rather suffer wrong than scream and fight, she goes on with her work, telling Charlie that he is a very naughty boy and making the very common remark that she thinks there never were such troublesome children as hers!

Now, who cannot see the different effect it would have had on these children if that mother had taken the trouble to make them realise and confess their fault, and voluntarily exchange the kiss of reconciliation and brotherly affection? What if it had taken half an hour of her precious time, would not the gain be greater than that which would accrue from any other occupation, however important? Mothers, if you want your children to walk in the way they should go, you must not only teach, you must be at the trouble to train.

Another important point in training a child in the way he should go is to train it in the practice of truth and integrity. Human nature is said to go 'astray from the womb-speaking lies' and, doubtless, untruthfulness is one of the most easily besetting and prevalent sins of our race. To counteract this tendency, and to establish the soul in habits of truth and sincerity, must be one of the first objects of right training.

In order to do this, parents should beware of palliating or excusing the tendency to falsehood in their children. In nothing have I been more amazed than in this. I have actually seen mothers smile at and almost extol the little artifices of their children in their attempts to deceive them and to hide some childish delinquency. No wonder that such parents fail to inspire their offspring with that wholesome dread of falseness which is one of the greatest safeguards to virtue in after life.

No mother will succeed in begetting in her child a greater antipathy towards any sin than she feels for it herself. Children are the quickest of all analysts, and instinctively detect in a moment all affectation of goodness. They judge not so much from what we say as how we feel. They are not influenced so much by our teaching as by our spirit and example.

For instance, a mother teaches her child that he is to be truthful, and on no account to tell a lie; but what effect will such teaching have if he hears her tell one, or sees her act one, the next day? Parents teach their children to be sincere, and take occasion to point out examples of the meanness and wickedness of deception, but by their own example they very frequently train them in the grossest insincerity.

Take an illustration. A person calls to see you whose society your child knows that you neither esteem nor desire, but you are all smiles and compliments, pressing her to come again, and assuring her that her visit has given you very great pleasure. What more effectual lesson could you give your wondering little one in deception and double-dealing than this?

And yet how common is this kind of thing in many households? I once stayed in the house of a lady who had a fine promising boy of about 18 months old. He used to kick and scream violently when he found that she was going out of the house. This, of course, was the result of previous bad training. But what did she do? Instead of facing the difficulty, and in a calm, firm, and affectionate manner curing her little son of this bad habit, she used to promise every time that she would bring him a pony that he could ride on, and the little fellow believed and believed until he got tired, and then put down his mother, in his baby mind, as a liar. Of course he would not have understood such a definition, but the deception would be burned into his soul never to be eradicated. A child hurts himself against the table: the mother strikes it, and says, 'Oh! naughty table! You have hurt baby', but the child soon learns that the table was not to blame, and at the same time learns to distrust his mother, who said it was.

A mother invites some little friends to spend an afternoon with her children, during which games are played requiring skill and tact in the winner. Her little boy wins several of the games, and although his brother or one of his little friends says that he was not fair – that is, that he cheated – she does not appear to notice it, but contents herself by saying, 'Oh, you must be good children and not quarrel', thus inflicting an unjust reflection on the child of honour and integrity, while encouraging the other in the meanest and most selfish form of sin, allowing him to rejoice over the victory won, through fraud or sleight-of-hand. Can such a mother wonder if her boy turns out a thief or a gambler?

Well, but you say how unpleasant it would be in such a case to go into particular investigation, spoil the enjoyment of the party and expose your child as a cheat before them! Certainly it would be very unpleasant, and to a mother who is more concerned about her son appearing to be a cheat than she is about his being one the result would not be worth the fuss; but, to a mother who esteems the honour and integrity of her boy more than all appearances or opinions in the world, such an opportunity of correcting his fault and fortifying him against future temptation is more than the breaking up of a dozen parties.

Oh, how many a promising child has been ruined because his mother would not endure the pain and trouble of an investigation? 'He that covereth his sins shall not prosper.' Neither does such a course win the good opinion of others. The children go away feeling that your son is a cheat just the same; and, what is worse, feeling that you are a party to his wickedness.

Again, Charlie is ill, and it is needful for him to take a dose of unpleasant medicine; but he has been so badly trained that his mother knows he will not take it if she tells him it is nasty. So she resorts to stratagem, and tells him that she has got something good, and thus coaxes him to take it into his mouth. But before it is swallowed he detects the cheat, and medicine and mother's veracity are spit out together. In this way thousands of children are taught deception and untruth, and you may labour in vain in after years to make them truthful and sincere. The soil has been ruined by early abuse.

Mothers, if you want your child to be truthful and sincere you must not only teach it to be so, you must be so yourself, and see that your child practises what you teach. You must not wink at, or cover up any kind of falseness or deception in him, because he is yours. Sin should be the more awful to you because you see it in those so dear, and those for whom you are responsible. If you have any reason to suspect your child of insincerity or falsehood, do not rest until you have bottomed the matter; never mind what trouble or pain it involves, drag it out, even though it should bring for the time exposure and disgrace. This may prove a useful chastisement, and a warning in the future.

Anything is preferable to sin covered up, and consequently encouraged. Resolve that you will make your child truthful and sincere, if you can do it no other way, from very despair of being able to hide anything from you. God acts on this principle with adults: why should not we with our children? 'Be sure your sin will find you out.'

I know some children amongst whom it is a common remark, 'It is of no use trying to hide anything from Mamma, for she is sure to find it out; so it is best to tell her at once.' How much misery it would save if it were thus in every family! Mothers, take the trouble to make your children true, and

God will enable you to do it. If you work for him with your children, he will work with you in them, and you shall have the joy of seeing them grow up into Christ, their living Head in all things.

But further. To train a child in the way it should go, we must not stop with those qualities and virtues which bear on man; but it must be trained in the exercise of devotion and piety towards God.

Of course, none but truly Christian parents are equal to impart this kind of training. The Holy Ghost must needs be in the heart of the mother who undertakes to lead her child to God. The bias to evil is too strong to be turned aside by unassisted human wisdom or strength, however great. But, bless God! there is every encouragement to those parents who are truly his, to hope for success in training their children for him.

And, perhaps, the first important point in such effort is, to lead our children to regard themselves as standing in a special relationship to God. 'The promise is to you and to your children.'

There is a sense in which the children of believers are already set apart for him. Many parents seem to lose sight of this covenant relationship, and bring up their children under the idea that they must needs live in sin till they come to be 15 or 16 years old, and then they hope God will convert them in the same marvellous and sudden manner in which drunkards and profligates are converted. Now, I am as firm a believer in conversion as anyone can be, and I also believe that the children of believers need to be converted as much as others, but I say this is not the way to teach our children to expect it.

What is conversion but the renewal of the mind by the Holy Ghost through faith in a crucified Saviour? And as there are 'diversities of operations by the same Spirit', why may not the minds of children be renewed very early? Why may they not be led to choose Christ and his yoke at seven or eight years old as well as at 17? If the will of a child be sincerely yielded to God, cannot the blessed Spirit as easily and as effectually renew and actuate its heart and affections as those of an adult? And does not Jesus say, 'Suffer the little ones to come unto me'? Alas! How many Christian parents unwittingly forbid them?

Because in the case of those who have had no previous light or training, conversion is necessarily sudden and followed by a great outward change, is that any reason why in the case of a child carefully trained in the 'nurture and admonition of the Lord', the Holy Spirit should not work together with such training, adapting his operations to the capacity and requirements of the little ones who are already 'of the Kingdom of Heaven', thus gradually installing them in all the privileges, duties and enjoyments of that Kingdom?

Of what advantage would it be to train them in the 'nurture and admonition of the Lord' if he did not purpose to bless this training to their conversion and salvation? The very terms of this injunction show the sense in which the Holy Spirit uses them. 'Nurture' means 'nursing, feeding, strengthening, developing'. 'Admonition' means 'reproof, caution, instruction'. Here is the order of God: firstly, the feeding and strengthening of all that is good in them; secondly, the reproof and caution against evil; and thirdly, instruction in righteousness.

If parents would only take the Lord's way they would see their sons and daughters taking their places in the temple of the Lord as their natural and abiding home. Wisely and faithfully trained up for God, they would say, when solicited to go away, 'To whom shall we go?'

'Ah,' says some mother, 'it is very easy to talk, but you don't know the natural antipathy which my children have to religion. I am sure I have tried to teach them the right way, and to make them love that which is good, but, so far, I see very little result of my labours.'

Perhaps, my friend, the failure has been in that you have taught but have not trained. You have told them the way to take, but have not led them in it. If you are to succeed you must do both, and that continually.

Of course right training includes right teaching, for though there may be much teaching without training, there cannot be good training without teaching. Doubtless many parents and teachers fail here for want of tact and wisdom in their methods of instruction.

The one great rule to be observed in all teaching is to make your lessons interesting. If you cannot awaken the interest of your child, you had better give up, and school and inform yourself till you can. Have not a doubt that many an impetuous, earnest, high-spirited child is driven to hate the Bible, the sanctuary and religious exercises in general by the cold, spiritless, insipid, canting manner in which he hears them read and performed. He knows by instinct that this is not the way people go through things in which their hearts are deeply concerned. He hears father and mother and friends talk in a natural, easy, interesting manner on business and family matters and consequently he listens with interest, but the moment they begin with religion he feels there is no heart in it, he feels that it is because they must, and not because they like.

He is taught to sing 'Happy, happy Sunday, the brightest of the seven' but he knows that in his home it is the dullest day of the week, and that the whole household are relieved when it is passed and they are able to be back at this world's employments and enjoyments.

Now, if you want your child to love and enjoy the Sabbath you must make it the most interesting day of the week. If you want him to love and read his Bible you must so tell him its stories, and elucidate its lessons as to make it interest him. If you want him to love prayer you must so pray as to interest and draw out his mind and heart with your own, and teach him to go to God, as he comes to you, in his own natural voice and manner to tell him his wants and to express his joys or sorrows. The themes of religion are of all themes most interesting to children when dealt with naturally and interestingly.

I used to take my eldest boy on my knee from the time when he was about two years old and tell him the stories of the Old Testament in baby language and adapted to baby comprehension, one at a time, so that he thoroughly drank them in and also the moral lessons they were calculated to convey. When between three and four years old I remember once going into the nursery and finding him mounted on his rocking horse, in a high state of excitement, finishing the story of Joseph to his nurse and baby brother, showing them how Joseph galloped on his live 'gee gee' when he went to fetch his father to show him to Pharaoh. In the same way we subsequently went through the history of the flood, having a Noah's ark, which was kept for Sabbath use, making the ark itself the foundation of one lesson, Noah and his family of another, and the gathering of the animals of a third, and so on until the subject was exhausted.

When my family increased, it was my custom before these Sabbath lessons to have a short lively tune. A short prayer, in which I let them all repeat after me, sentence by sentence, asking the Lord to help us to understand his Word and to bless our souls, and so on. After the lesson another short prayer, and then another tune or two. After this they would adjourn to the nursery, where frequently they would go through the whole service again, the eldest being the preacher. When baby was asleep their nurse would read interesting infantile stories to the elder ones, or teach them suitable bits of poetry by letting them all repeat it together after her. Thus the Sabbath was made a day of pleasure as well as of instruction and improvement.

I never allowed my children to attend public services till they were old enough to take some interest in them. We had no mission services then, or they would have been able to understand, and enter into a great part of them, but I deemed it an evil to make a child sit still for an hour-and-a-half, dangling its legs on a high seat, listening to what it could neither understand nor appreciate, for alas, there is little in the ordinary services of our day to interest or profit children, and I am satisfied that a great deal of the distaste for religious services so common amongst them has been engendered in this way. My experience has been that my children have come so highly to appreciate the privilege of attending service, that a promise of it during the week would insure extra good behaviour and diligence.

Of course, mothers who have no one to leave with their children cannot always stay at home, and must take them as often as is necessary for their own edification. To those parents who are able to keep servants I would say, make any sacrifice to keep a really good Christian girl with your children. I have made it a rule never to have any other as a nurse, and have sometimes put up with great inexperience and incompetency, because it was associated with goodness. Better take a girl whom you have to teach how to wash a child's face, or to stitch a button on, if she is true and sincere, than have one ever so clever who will teach your children to lie and deceive.

But to return to the subject of teaching, not only must you make your teaching interesting, but also practical, in the highest degree. Your children want to know how to comport themselves now in the little duties, trials and enjoyments of their daily life. It is to be feared that, as with adults so with children, a deal of so-called teaching is right away above their heads, dealing with abstract truths and far-off illustrations, instead of coming down to such everyday matters as obedience to parents and teachers; the learning of their lessons; their treatment of brothers, sisters, and servants; their companionships; their amusements; the spending and giving of their pocket money; their dealings with the poor; their treatment of animals – in short, everything embraced in their daily life.

The great end of Christian training is to lead children to realise the fact that they belong to God and are under a solemn obligation to do everything in a way which they think will please him. Parents cannot begin too early, nor labour too continuously, to keep this fact before the minds of their children.

In the family devotion in the morning, the father or mother, or whoever conducts it, should bring the children specially before the Lord, asking him to give them grace this day, to be obedient to those who have the care of them, to be diligent at their lessons, so that they may lay in knowledge, which shall make them useful to their fellow-creatures, and enable them to do something for God and souls, if he sees fit to spare them.

Above all things, parents should labour to counteract the natural selfishness of the hearts of their children by showing them that they are not to live unto themselves. That they are not to be good, and industrious, and studious in order that they themselves may be learned, or happy, or successful in the world, for these are the things after which the Gentiles – the unbelieving world – seek, but that they, as belonging to God, are to live unto him, who hath given himself for them, seeking first his Kingdom and righteousness. Seeking first to glorify him, and do good to their generation, leaving it with him to fix the bounds of their habitation, and to choose their inheritance for them.

Alas! How few Christian parents seem to understand this first principle of right training, hence their anxiety to push their children on, and up, in the learning, principles, customs and ambitions of this world. Surely 'God is not mocked', for as they 'sow to the flesh' they 'of the flesh reap corruption' and alas! their poor children's souls are sacrificed in the bargain.

Oh, mothers, don't be deceived – if you want your children to be the Lord's when they grow up, if you want your boy to withstand the unknown temptations of the future, if you want him to come out a man of righteous principle, integrity and honour, superior to all the doubleness, chicanery and devilry of the world, you must train him to look upon all the world's prizes as dross compared with the joy of a pure conscience and a life of usefulness to his fellow-men.

If you want your daughter to be a true woman, willing to sacrifice and to suffer in the interests of humanity and truth, you must inspire her now with a contempt for the baubles for which so many women barter their lives and their souls. You must teach her that she is an independent, responsible being, whom God will call to as severe a reckoning for the use or abuse of her talents as that of her brother man. Day by day, as it flies, you must labour to wake up your children's souls to the realisation of the fact that they belong to God, and that he has sent them into the world not to look after their own little petty, personal interests but to devote themselves to the promotion of his, and that, in doing this, they will find happiness, usefulness, and glory (see Matthew 25:14-16).

I would like, in conclusion, to add a few cautions against evils which I have seen to be very common in families, and which I believe exert a very baneful influence on the formation of character. First amongst these is an inordinate estimate of the value of money. One would think from the meanness and the discomfort of the ordering of many families that money was the household god at whose shrine every consideration of comfort, health, friendship and benevolence had been sacrificed. 'What will it cost?' is the first question that meets every suggestion of improvement in any direction, and this frequently, not because money is scarce, but simply because it cannot be parted with!

Now children soon find out the ruling principle in the family administration, and if they see it to be covetousness, or avariciousness, parents may teach all the catalogue of Christian virtues from morning till night, but their children will grow up selfish in the very core of their souls. Like begets like the world over. You show me a household where the spirit of covetousness reigns and I will show you ungenerous, cunning children.

'The love of money is the root of all evil' is an axiom as true as it is neglected, and until parents, by their actions, show their children that they deem domestic comfort and religion, the claims of Christian hospitality, the blood and lives of their servants, the claims of the suffering and the destitute, and the crying need of the benighted multitude, of more importance than the hoarding of money they must go on reaping the reward of their covetousness in the selfish indulgence, ungrateful neglect and open profligacy of their children. Ah, how many a parent, who has sacrificed all the higher and nobler impulses of his own and his children's natures to money-making has had it scattered by wicked, selfish sons!

Another great evil which I have seen even in families where there has, in the main, been much good training, is the yielding in an emergency on points of principle for the sake of expediency. Take an illustration. Here is a family who are trained in the principles of abstinence from intoxicating drinks, as all Christian families undoubtedly ought to be. These parents have wisely taught their children that strong drink is an evil and bitter thing, and that all traffic and countenance of it brings a curse; but on a certain day, a letter comes announcing that General So-and-so, or Captain Somebody is coming to pay a visit to his cousin, on his return from India.

Of course there is much excitement and expectation among the junior members of the family, and a becoming anxiety on the part of the parents, worthily to entertain their guest. But a difficulty presents itself. The general is not an abstainer. He has always been accustomed to his wine and spirits. 'What shall we do?' says the mother. 'He will think it inhospitable and mean to deny him his favourite beverage.'

'Well, yes,' says the father. 'I don't see how we can do it in this instance. You see he is an old man, and would not appreciate our views or our motives. I fear we shall have to order a little wine for him. I don't like to bring it in sight of the children, but we must explain the circumstances to them, and we will hope no harm will come of it.'

These parents sacrifice principle to expediency, and admit the mocker to their family circle. Can they be surprised if one of their sons turns out a drunkard?

'Ah!' said a broken-hearted father once to my husband. 'I trained my boy in abstinence principles, but I did not keep him out of the society of those who thought there was no harm in moderate drinking, and now he is an outcast and an alien whom I cannot allow to cross my threshold. He has killed his mother, and will bring down my grey hairs with sorrow to the grave.'

Have no fellowship with the unfruitful works or instruments of evil. Wine is a mocker. Wine itself, not the abuse of it. Here is the secret why so many thousands of the fair and promising fall by it. Christian parents, fear it as you would the bite of a serpent, and as you value the souls or your children keep it out of their very sight.

Another great enemy to the formation of righteous character is ambition for what is called position in society! Some parents are continually putting before their children future aggrandisement and fortune, as a stimulus to industry and effort, thus holding up to their young minds this world's prosperity and applause as the great aim and object of life. To get to be more learned, more genteel, more wealthy than men of their own class, so that they may be received into higher circles of worldly society.

Such parents often fail, and in the attempt to leap the chasm which bars his upward course, many a son falls headlong through the abyss of disappointed ambition, down to damnation, and many a daughter to that path, the steps of which 'take hold on hell'. Ah, but some succeed! Yes, and what reward do the parents often get? The son and daughter, whom they toiled and struggled so hard to push up, get so high they can scarcely see the poor, neglected parents down below, and often leave them to die in poverty, and with a broken heart. Truly 'Godliness with contentment is great gain'.

I cannot close these remarks without lifting up my voice against the practice, now so prevalent amongst respectable families, of sending children to boarding schools before their principles are formed or their characters developed. Parents are led away by the professedly religious character of schools, forgetting that, even supposing the master or governess may be all that can be desired, a school is a little world where all the elements of unrenewed human nature are at work with as great variety, subtlety and power as in the great world outside. You would shrink from exposing your child to the temptation and danger of association with unconverted worldly men and women, why should you expose them to the influence of children of the same character, who are not infrequently sent to these schools because they have become utterly vitiated and unmanageable at home?

I have listened to many a sad story of the consequences of these school associations, and early made up my mind to keep my children under my own influence, at least until they had attained that maturity in grace and principle which would be an effectual safeguard against ungodly associations. To this end I have rejected several very tempting offers in the way of educational advantage, and every day I am increasingly thankful for having been enabled to do so. God has laid on you, parents, the responsibility of training your children, and you cannot possibly delegate that responsibility to another without endangering their highest interests for time and for eternity.

Two

Worldly amusement and Christianity

WE are constantly meeting with persons in perplexity as to how far they may participate in worldly amusements without compromising their Christian profession. Many confess having been for years in controversy on the subject of attending or assisting at concerts, penny readings and gatherings of a similar, though more private and social character, and not a few have admitted having suffered spiritual loss and declension through being mixed up with such entertainments.

On this question there seems to be amongst the Lord's professing people a sad indefiniteness of view. Indeed, many appear to have no settled convictions on the subject. Hence, we fear, arises much of the abounding worldliness that prevails in the Church, and hence the extinction of the demarcation line between so many thousands of the professing Christians of our day and the ungodly throngs around them.

We propose briefly in this paper to consider, first is it lawful, and secondly is it expedient for Christians either to provide or attend such entertainments as penny readings, concerts, private theatricals and the like?

Firstly, is it lawful? To the law and to the testimony: what saith the Scriptures?

'For thou art an holy people unto the Lord thy God; the Lord thy God hath chosen thee to be a special people unto himself, above all the people that are upon the face of the earth' (Deuternonomy 7:6). 'And ye shall be holy unto me: for I the Lord am holy, and have severed you from other people, that ye should be mine' (Leviticus 20:26). 'Be not conformed to this world; but be ye transformed by the renewing of your mind, that ye may prove what is that good and acceptable and perfect will of God' (Romans 12:2). 'If ye were of the world, the world would love his own; but because ye are not of the world, therefore the world hateth you' (John 15:19). 'For all that is in the world, the lust of the eyes, and the pride of life is not of the Father, but is of the world' (1 John 2:16). 'Wherefore come out from among them, and be ye separate, saith the Lord, and touch not the unclean thing: and I will receive you, and will be a Father unto you, and ye shall be my sons and daughters, saith the Lord Almighty' (2 Corinthians 6:17, 18). 'Whosoever therefore will be the friend of the world is the enemy of God' (James 4:4).

We presume that all Christians attach some meaning to such passages as these; but one says they do not apply to this worldly custom, and another says they do not apply to that, until, as in the case of the Mahometan pig, the whole is swallowed, and every worldly-minded professor manages to get the piece he likes best, or which appears most to his interest: thus the law of Christ is frittered away, and the whole body of his professing Church given over to the god of this world. What then is the conformity to, and friendship with, the world, which these and a host of similar passages prohibit? In other words, what is worldliness?

We reply: firstly, we take that to be worldly which professes to be so. Neither men nor things are, as a rule, better than they profess to be. Secondly, we take that to be worldly which, in sentiment and spirit, the children of the world love, esteem, and enjoy. Thirdly, we count whatever has no reference to God, righteousness, or eternity, which 'savoureth not of the things of God', as worldly. Fourthly, everything that is adverse in spirit to the dignity, gravity and usefulness of the Christian character we regard as worldly.

It seems to us that these propositions are so self-evident that no thoughtful Christian can gainsay them. Some professors seem to regard nothing as worldly which is not absolutely devilish – such as profanity, blasphemy or obscenity. But the Scriptures carefully and clearly distinguish between the two. They prohibit Christians conforming to the world in the habits and usages of daily life.

They are not to talk like the world, in the way of foolish jesting, 'swelling words', etc. But, on the contrary, their conversation is to 'be seasoned with salt', meet to 'minister grace to the hearers'. It is to be 'pure', proceeding from 'a good' (not a doubtful) 'conscience'. It is to be 'in Heaven, from whence we look for the appearing of our Lord Jesus Christ'.

The Scriptures prohibit Christians dressing like the world. 'Whose adorning let it not be that outward adorning of plaiting the hair, and of wearing of gold, or of putting on of apparel' (1 Peter 3:3). 'In like manner also, that women adorn themselves in modest apparel, with shamefacedness and sobriety, not with braided hair, or gold, or pearls, or costly array; but, which becometh women professing godliness, with good works' (1 Timothy 2:9, 10). 'Moreover the Lord saith, because the daughters of Zion are haughty, and walk with stretched forth necks and wanton eyes, walking and mincing as they go: therefore the Lord will smite with a scab the crown of the head of the daughters of Zion' (Isaiah 3:16, 17). We commend this whole chapter to the consideration of all whom it may concern, and we would suggest that as the Lord Jehovah regarded the dress of those Israelitish women as a sign of their backslidden condition, and thought it sufficiently important to be recorded by his holy prophet, it may be well for us to consider how far the same signs are manifest amongst us in our day.

The Scriptures prohibit Christians singing the songs of the world, for they expressly enjoin that when they are merry or glad they are to sing psalms and make melody in their heart unto the Lord.

The Scriptures prohibit Christians from joining in the amusements of the world, forbidding any fellowship with the unfruitful works of darkness, commanding to abstain from the very appearance of evil, and to come out from amongst the ungodly and be separate; and our Lord declared that his real disciples were not of the world, even as he was not of the world.

Now in the light of these Scriptures, and of the propositions we have laid down, let us examine the character of some of the entertainments so popular with many professing Christians.

We find that it is no uncommon thing for entertainments to be held in private drawing-rooms and in rooms connected with churches and chapels, over which ministers and leading men in churches preside, at which Shakespearian readings are given, with extracts from the works of the most popular and worldly novelists, and the same songs sung as are echoed and applauded in the public house and the dancing-room.

Now, viewed in the light of the Scriptures we have quoted and tried by the propositions we have drawn from them, how do these practices strike you, Christian reader?

Firstly, are they not professedly worldly? Do they not savour of the world, all of the world, and of the world only? Were not the authors of the things said and sung at such entertainments thoroughly Christless men, and some of them professed infidels?

Secondly, are not these the songs and sentiments which worldlings have always claimed as their own? Are they not sung in their ballrooms, theatres and casinos? And is not this proof enough that they are congenial to their tastes, and in keeping with their spirit?

Thirdly, such songs, recitations and performances have no reference whatever to God, righteousness or eternity. God is not only 'not in all their thoughts', but he is not in any of them, therefore they must be thoroughly worldly.

Fourthly, the spirit of such amusements is manifestly adverse to the dignity, gravity and usefulness of the Christian character. What are its effects? Lightness, foolish jesting, a false estimate of creature delights, obtuseness to spiritual things, and frequently uproarious merriment and godless mirth.

We put it to any Christian who has ever allowed himself to take part in such amusements whether these are not their inevitable and bitter fruits, and whether he has not found their spirit to be utterly antagonistic to the spirit of Christ? We have heard many backsliders in heart attribute their declension to mingling in such scenes of folly and frivolity, and we never met with one whom we had reason to believe had been renewed in the spirit of his mind who could say he could enter into them without condemnation.

Doubtless there are thousands of professing Christians who live in perpetual strife with their consciences and with the Holy Spirit on this subject; and verily they have their reward. Trying to hold Christ in one hand and the world in the other, they lose both. They have no joy in their godless amusements, neither have they any joy in the Lord. All is darkness, condemnation, and death. 'Ye adulterers and adulteresses, know ye not that the friendship of the world is enmity with God?'

The testimony of the Word is too explicit, and the voice of the Spirit too clear, for any child of God to err for want of light if he will but listen to his divine counsellor. But, alas! too many seek to silence his voice by vain and worldly reasoning, lowering the standard which he has given them because somebody else does so. They do not hear him saying, 'What is that to thee? Follow thou me ... Love not the world, neither the things of the world. If any man love the world the love of the Father is not in him.'

Not only is the testimony of the Word and of the Spirit against these amusements, but the testimony and example of the most devoted and intelligent Christians of all ages have been against them. The following are a few extracts bearing on the subject.

'There is no earthly pleasure which has not the inseparable attendance of grief, and that following it as closely as Jacob came after Esau. Yea, worldly delight is but a shadow; and when we catch after it, all that we grasp is substantial sorrow in its room. The honey should not be very delightful, when the sting is so near' (Alleine).

'If there be any sorceress upon earth it is pleasure; which so enchanteth the minds of men, and worketh the disturbance of our peace with such secret delight, that foolish men think this want of tranquility happiness. She turneth man into swine with such sweet charms, that they would not change their brutish nature for their former reason' (Bishop Hall).

'Consider, this is not the season that should be for pleasure! The apostle James lays it as a great charge upon many in his time, that they lived in pleasure on earth. This is the time to do the great business for which we were born' (Ambrose).

'How often shall it be protested to the Christian world, by men of the greatest seriousness and devotion, that it is vain to dream of entering the Kingdom of Heaven hereafter, except the Kingdom of Heaven enter into their souls in this life! How long shall the Son of God, who came into the world to be the most glorious example of purity, self-denial, and mortification, how long shall he be by in his word as an antiquated pattern, only cut out for the apostolic ages, and only suited to some few morose and melancholy men? With what face can we pretend to true religion, or a feeling acquaintance with God, and the things of his Kingdom, whilst the continual bleatings and lowings of our souls after creature good betray us so manifestly, and proclaim before all the world, that the beast, the brutish life, is still so powerful in us?' (Shaw).

'I would that you should use this world as not abusing it, that you should be crucified to the world, and the world to you, that you should declare plainly that you seek a better country, which is an Heavenly. Ah! my dear brethren, I beseech you carry it like pilgrims and strangers, abstain from fleshly lusts which war against the soul; for what have we to do with the customs and fashions of this world, who are strangers in it? Be contented with travellers' lots; know you not that you are in a strange land?' (Joseph Alleine's *Letters*).

'I would dissuade thee from unnecessary society of ungodly men, and unprofitable companions, though they be not so apparently ungodly. It is not only the openly profane, the swearer, the drunkard, that will prove hurtful to us; but dead-hearted formalists, or persons merely civil and moral, or whose conference is empty, unsavoury, and barren, may much divert our thoughts from Heaven. As mere idleness and forgetting God will keep a soul as certainly from Heaven as a profane licentious life; so also will useless company as surely keep our hearts from Heaven' (Baxter).

'In speaking of the laws and limits of recreation, observe generally that whatever is offensive to God, whatever is injurious to others, whatever is hurtful, whether remotely or proximately to our own soul or body, is evil, to be avoided in ourselves and to be condemned in others. The principles involved in the foregoing remarks will answer the queries so frequently put. Is it right to frequent a theatre? To attend the ballroom? To sit at the card table? To mingle indiscriminately in gay and fashionable society? The study of the Bible quotations so largely made will furnish a reply. Read and you will know' (Samuel Martin).

'I bade farewell for ever to assemblies which I had visited, to plays and diversions, dancing, unprofitable walks and parties of pleasure. The amusements and pleasures, so much prized and esteemed by the world, now appeared to me dull and insipid; so much so, that I wondered how I ever could have enjoyed them' (Madame Guyon).

'I heard also that this new clergyman preached against all my favourite diversions, such as going to plays, reading novels, attending balls, assemblies, card tables, etc. I asked, "Is it true that he preaches against dancing?" I said I was resolved to take the first opportunity of conversing with him, being certain I could easily prove such amusements were not sinful. Being told what arguments he made use of, I revolved them in my mind, fully determined if I found upon reflection I could answer them, I would. I first considered if any Scripture example could be brought … but found nothing there which countenanced dancing in any measure. I then began to consider the objections urged against it. One of them was that as it tends to lively and trifling mirth, so it enervates the mind, dissipates the thoughts, weakens if not stifles serious and good impressions and quite indisposes the mind for prayer. I asked in my own mind, is not this a truth? Conscience answered in the affirmative. After much controversy, consideration and prayer she says: "For my own part I was conscious that it led me to dress and expenses not suited to my present situation in life. These thoughts brought powerful convictions to my mind, notwithstanding my desire to resist them. I could not deny that truth, in particular, that those who habitually attend such pleasures lose all relish for spiritual things. God is shut out of their thoughts and hearts; prayer, if they use any, is full of wanderings, or perhaps, wholly neglected; and death put as far as possible out of sight, lest the thought should spoil their pleasure."' (Mrs Rogers).

Did our space permit we could give hundreds of quotations of similar bearing by such writers as Augustine, Thomas a'Kempis, Luther, Knox, Howe, Leighton, Newton, Cecil, Henry, Locke, Bunyan, Whitfield, Wesley, Clarke, Barnes, Steir, Doddridge, Young and others. But our space prevents the calling of these witnesses. Christian reader, let those we have called suffice. 'As obedient children, not fashioning yourselves according to the former lusts in your ignorance, but as he which hath called you is holy, so ye be holy in all manner of conversation.'

Secondly, we come now to the question of expediency. The principal arguments brought forward by Christians in favour of providing and attending worldly amusements are: firstly, seeing that our young people will have amusement, it is better to provide them with that which is moral and comparatively innocent, than to drive them to that which is positively vicious. Secondly, seeing that we cannot get hold of the unconverted by the gospel, it is better to meet them halfway, and try, as it were, to catch them by guile.

These arguments look very plausible. Let us honestly consider them in the light of Scripture and actual experience.

Firstly, on whose behalf are they urged? Are the young people referred to the children of Christian parents, or the children of votaries of this world? If the latter, we reply that Christians are nowhere taught, either directly or indirectly, that it is any part of their duty to provide amusement for the children of this world; nay, the direct teaching and the whole tenor of Scripture go to prove that it is their duty to seek to alarm and convict them.

There is not a line in the whole Bible on which an argument can be built for amusing people while yet in their sins. The Scriptures ever represent the unconverted as under condemnation, in imminent danger, ready to be destroyed, a state rendering them far more fit objects for pity, concern and earnest Christian effort than for amusement. To keep them amused and self-satisfied is just what Satan desires, and all the better for his purpose if he can get it done by professed Christians.

Well but, say some of our expediency friends, if by getting unconverted young people to attend our penny readings, moral concerts and private parties where dancing, charades and such like pastimes are practised, we can show them that religion is not such a melancholy thing as they have imagined, and that to become Christians need not exclude them from such recreations, may we not hope so to induce them to attend our sanctuaries, and thus get them converted by our more direct Christian instrumentalities?

We answer, if you could thus promote good by doing evil, the end would fail to justify the means, for God says, 'To obey is better than sacrifice.' But there is the 'if' still undisposed of. We ask, does this worldly policy succeed? Do your evening parties, your miniature pantomimes, dancing, and song-singing lead to the conversion of our young people? Do the hotch-potch mixtures of Christ and Shakespeare, Paul and Dickens, of our times, serve to fill our sanctuaries and bring the people to Jesus?

Nay, verily, the crowds who will go fast enough to hear their favourite songs and flippant rhymes piped through the instruments of the temple on the weeknight, remorselessly leave those who have stooped to pander to their taste to chant the songs of Zion to empty pews on the Sabbath.

But supposing that in some instances worldlings are won by these means, what of all the mischief that is done? These amusements are pleaded for on the ground that they will save our young people from those of a vicious and immoral character, but we contend that they are quite as likely, in many instances, to pave the way to the vicious, as in others to save from it.

They will do this firstly by throwing over that which is purely sensuous and godless, and therefore sinful, the sanctity of association with Christ and religion. Secondly by lowering the standard of the purity and sanctity of the Christian character. Thirdly by destroying the respect and awe with which many of the unconverted have been accustomed to regard Christianity and Christian ministers. Fourthly by begetting a sense of security in sin, leading them to say, 'We cannot be so very far wrong, or these Christians would not associate with us, and find pleasure in our amusements. There is not so much difference between us after all.'

We fear that by these and similar means, the half-awakened conscience of many a young man and woman has been silenced and their hearts hardened; and instead of being won from vice, they have been driven faster into it. Alas, who can tell the convictions that are stifled, the serious impressions that are lost, the good resolutions that are scattered and the heavenly aspirations that are blasted in these religious pantomimes, these Christian-Belial festivities? Many sad stories come out, but eternity alone will reveal their full and awful consequences.

But the argument of expediency is not only urged on behalf of our unconverted young people, but (O tell it not in Gath!) also on behalf of the children of professing Christians! 'What are we to do?' say some professedly Christian parents. 'Our children must have recreation and amusement, and unless we allow them to mingle to some extent in fashionable society and attend such parties as you refer to, we must needs keep them out of society altogether and make recluses of them, for all our Christian friends patronise such entertainments and consider them innocent and lawful.'

If this be true, we reply, it reveals more clearly than anything we could say the backslidden and awful state of the professing Church, and calls loudly for some attempt to stem the tide of worldly comformity, while there remains a spark of spiritual life in her midst.

Alas, and has it come to pass that there is no strictly Christian social intercourse and enjoyment? Have the topics of our glorious Christianity become so stale and uninteresting? Have the themes of gospel enterprise and individual effort lost all their inspiration? Have the songs of Zion lost their enchanting and inspiriting influence? Has the voice of social prayer become quite silent? Has every spark of real enthusiasm in religion gone out, that when Christians want to find interest and enjoyment they must seek it in themes and things peculiarly belonging to the god of this world, and his votaries?

Has it come to pass that Christians have so little confidence in the God of the Bible, and the religion of Jesus, that they must seek an alliance between Christ and the world in order to interest their children and save them from open profligacy and vice? If so, how does this reflect on themselves? What sort of training does it imply? Have they trained their sons and daughters so truly in the spirit of the world, under the garb of a religious profession, that nothing but the most sensuous amusements of worldlings (who make any pretence to morality) will satisfy them?

Has it come to pass that the children of Christians must dress like harlots, dance, sing songs, read novels, attend concerts where worldly and even comic songs are sung, evoking uproarious laughter and unseemly jests, and all this for their amusement; their parents, and even ministers, looking on, and striving by the most blind and wicked perversion of the word of God, to justify their worldliness and salve their consciences? Alas, has it come to this? 'Oh that my head were waters, and mine eyes a fountain of tears, that I might weep day and night for the slain of the daughter of my people.'

Well, I think I hear some Christian say, 'What is to be done?' Done? Let everyone who has any convictions on this subject act on them. Half the mischief has resulted from Christians turning away from the simple teachings of the Word in order to pander to one another; 'measuring themselves amongst themselves', instead of measuring themselves by the standard of the Word.

We have heard them say, 'Well, I never felt quite satisfied that such things were right or consistent; but then, many far higher in Christian attainments than I am allow them; and it seems like condemning others, and making oneself to be holier than they.' Thus the voice of individual conscience has been stifled, and the standard gradually lowered, until Christ and Shakespeare are openly affianced, and Paul and Dickens bracketed together as equal benefactors of their race.

'But what am I to do?' is the still recurring cry of some timid Christian mother or father. 'Must I keep my children out of society altogether?' Yes, verily, if you cannot find any truly Christian society for them. Humble yourself deeply before God for having trained your children with worldly tastes and associations, and set yourself, as far as possible, to remedy the evil. Get more spirituality, more real life, and you will find your religion astonishingly more interesting both to yourself and to your children.

'Well, but my children must have companions.' Oh, no, there is no must in the case; better live without them than have such as lead them away from God and into friendship with the world. If you have not yet learnt this, I fear you have never realised your responsibility to God for your children's souls.

Do you regard your children as your own or the Lord's? If your own, you will train them on worldly principles; but if the Lord's, you will surely train them for him, that they may serve their generation according to his will. You have nothing to do with consequences, it is yours to obey. God will take care of his own. Act on your convictions of duty. If you stand alone in your family, your circle, your church – never mind. Act for yourself, as you must give account for yourself. Perhaps, if you make a beginning, somebody else will follow. Somebody must begin; somebody must make a stand. Why not you?

You say, 'I am so uninfluential, so weak, and the cross will be so heavy.' All the more blessing in carrying it; and he who chooses the weak things will bless your testimony, and use it for his glory. Only honour God, and he will honour you.

But I must hasten to consider the second argument urged in support of this expediency Christianity: 'Seeing that the gospel fails to attract our young people, it is better to meet them halfway and try, as it were, to catch them by guile.'

We reply: is the success of the gospel dependent on worldly expediency or on spiritual power? If on the former, we can see the force of this argument; but if on the latter, it is utterly irrelevant. There are but two kinds of influence or power in operation in the Church: the material and the spiritual. Jesus Christ utterly and continually abjured the material as being of any value in his Kingdom.

He systematically ignored, both by example and precept, all the influence of mere learning, traditional religion, wealth, position, worldly power and policy, and steadily maintained that his Kingdom was not 'of this world'. He solemnly abjured all other kinds of influence or power save that of the divine, and laboured incessantly to imbue his disciples with the conviction that nothing short of this endowment could empower them for their work (Acts 1:4, 5; Luke 14:48, 49; John 15).

We all know how completely Paul and his fellow apostles learnt this lesson, and how they continually gloried in the testimony that it was 'not by might nor by power, but by the Spirit of the Lord' that they did all their wonderful works. While the early Christians were true to the example and teaching of their Master, we never find them bemoaning their lack of ability to attract or to convert the people. So mighty was their influence, though comparatively few in number, and insignificant in social position, that wherever they went they were said to have 'turned the world upside down', and large and flourishing churches sprang up in all directions.

They did not feel the necessity for any halfway meeting place between themselves and the world. They did not lower the tone of their Christian morality in order to meet the corrupt and heathenish notions of those around them. Neither did they abjure their spirituality lest it should disgust them. On the contrary, the apostles and early

Christians seem to have had the conviction that the more complete their devotion to their Master, the more separate from the world, the more truly spiritual and divine they were, the greater would be their influence for God, and the greater their success in winning men to Christ.

It never seems to have entered into their minds to descend from the high vantage ground on which their Lord had placed them, to fight the enemy with his own weapons and to try to cast him out by a partial conformity to his darling lusts (1 John 2:16). The source of their power was divine, therefore they needed no adjuncts of human policy or of worldly expediency.

They were mighty 'through God' and could well dispense with the heathen poets and fashionable novelists of their times. Their preaching was with the 'demonstration of the Spirit and of power', consequently multitudes listened, believed and turned to the Lord.

It was not until the primitive Christians began to admit worldly principles of action, and to substitute the material for the spiritual, that their influence began to wane, and their testimony to lose its power. It was the gradual substitution of the human for the divine, the material for the spiritual, that overspread Christendom for ages with papal darkness and death. During that long night of error and suffering, however, God raised up many witnesses to the sufficiency of the Holy Ghost to attract and convert men; many making long pilgrimages and suffering great privations in order to visit and converse with those endued with this divine gift.

And when at length the light of the Reformation broke over the nations, this one great lesson was again engraven on the hearts of God's chosen instruments: 'Not by might, nor by power, but by my Spirit, saith the Lord of Hosts!' Thus, after the lapse of ages, we find the gospel, when preached with the old power, the same mighty instrumentality, both for attracting the multitudes and converting the soul.

From the Reformation down to the present time, we find that wherever the same gospel has been preached with the same accompanying power, the same results have followed, even when the preacher has been trammelled by a false creed, or beset with hosts of opposing influences from earth and hell. Where the Spirit of the Lord is, there spiritual miracles are wrought, and wherever miracles are wrought, the people will congregate; be it by the riverside, in the temple, in kirk, church, chapel, theatre, meeting-house, attic or cellar. There is no quicker detective of the presence of the Spirit of Jesus than the spirit which worketh in the hearts of the children of disobedience. But he has always been more than a match for would-be exorcists. 'Jesus I know, and Paul I know, but who are ye?'

You will perceive, Christian reader, that we regard this plea, that 'the gospel fails to attract', as a very suspicious one. We ask those who urge it, in the light of the foregoing summary of facts, to tell us why it fails. We have no hesitation in saying only for want of the Holy Ghost. The great desideratum in connection with all our organisations, societies, churches, agencies and instrumentalities is life, life, life! The people want a living gospel, preached by living Spirit-baptised souls. Dare we, in the light of the past, instead of this divine bread give them the stone of materialism? If so, we must prepare for the consequences.

Three

Heart backsliding

REVELATION 2:1-5: 'Unto the angel of the church of Ephesus write: These things saith he that holdeth the seven stars in his right hand, who walketh in the midst of the seven golden candlesticks. I know thy works and thy labour, and thy patience, and how thou canst not bear them which are evil; and thou hast tried them which say they are apostles, and are not, and hast found them liars. And hast borne, and hast patience, and for my name's sake hast laboured and hast not fainted. Nevertheless I have somewhat against thee, because thou hast left thy first love. Remember therefore, from whence thou art fallen, and repent, and do the first works; or else I will come unto thee quickly, and will remove thy candlestick out of his place, except thou repent.'

As introductory to my remarks on this passage, I want you to observe that this is a direct message from Christ himself to a company of his own people in a certain state of religious experience. These Ephesians were Christians, born into the family of God, and for a long time, and to a great extent, had faithfully served him.

Hear what he says of them in this second verse: 'I know thy works, and thy labour, and thy patience, and how thou canst not bear them which are evil; and thou hast tried them which say they are apostles, and are not, and hast found them liars; and hast borne, and hast patience, and for my name's sake hast laboured, and hast not fainted.'

He sums up their character most carefully, giving them the utmost credit for all the fruits of the Spirit found in them, He remembers their labour, their patience, their hatred of evil, their zeal for his glory in their intolerance of false teachers, their constancy in suffering, their purity of motive, and their continuance in well doing. Not one of their good deeds is forgotten before him; but the brilliancy and preciousness of the whole is marred by one defect which only he could see, but which his love and faithfulness compelled him to reveal and to reprove: 'Nevertheless I have somewhat against thee, because thou hast left thy first love.'

After such a repetition of their fidelities and graces, we, in our carnal wisdom, might have looked for a therefore instead of a nevertheless. We might have expected him to say, 'Thou hast laboured for me with much zeal, patience and perseverance; therefore I will excuse and pass over thy declension in love, thy defection of heart.' This is the way in which many of God's people seem to imagine that he regards heart unfaithfulness; but not so the Lord himself. Notwithstanding all their labours, sufferings, patience and zeal, he had a nevertheless against them, which compelled his reproof and endangered his anger.

And oh, is not this his attitude towards thousands of his people now? Is not this message to these Ephesian Christians equally applicable to multitudes in our day, who are serving him with much zeal and patience but they have left their first love and are, notwithstanding all their outward professions and labour, backsliders in heart?

Some of you start at the use of such a phrase, and you say, 'But these Ephesians were not backsliders.' Not in the general acceptation of the term, but in the estimation of their Lord they were backsliders in heart. They had partially fallen, partially gone from that wholehearted service which once they rendered him, and without which all outward works, however worthy or zealous, will not suffice.

I fear that after this manner the great majority of Christians are backsliders. I have conversed with numbers up and down this land, and many who have occupied prominent positions in Christian churches, who have confessed that they were secret backsliders, having lost much that they once enjoyed, and walking far less carefully than they once did. Taking these as representatives of others in similar circumstances, I say I cannot but fear that a very large majority of professing Christians have, like these Ephesian converts, left their first love. I have no doubt that there are many of this class here this morning, and I desire to speak especially to these.

Let me entreat you, my dear friends, to open your hearts to the reception of the truth. Forget the feeble instrumentality through which it comes, and, if it commends itself to your consciences as God's truth, let it have its full weight upon your hearts. If you are right, it will do you no harm to examine yourselves. It will establish you and help you 'to assure your hearts before him'. And if you are not right, who can tell the importance of making the discovery in time, while there is opportunity and grace offered by which you may be made right?

I beseech you, be honest with yourselves and with God. There is nothing to be gained by crying, 'Peace, peace' when there is no peace. It is no use trying to persuade yourselves that you are right with God if your consciences tell you that you are not. You will find your consciousness too strong for all the false theories of men and devils, and true peace will be impossible to you until you come back to your first love.

I think I hear someone say, 'Ah! That is just what I want, but how am I to do it? I know that I am a backslider in heart; it is not with me now as it once was; but I have tried and tried in vain to get back what I once enjoyed, and to live as I once lived.'

My dear friend, you have not tried in the right way. Try your Lord's way; take his council, obey his commands, and you shall not only get back all you have lost, but an abundant increase of peace and power.

This way, as pointed our here, seems to me to be: firstly, remember; realise your unfaithfulness. Secondly, repent; humble yourself, confess and renounce your sin. Thirdly, do your first works: consecration and faith.

Remember; realise your unfaithfulness. Remember from whence thou art fallen. There are different degrees of backsliding; some have fallen from greater heights, and some to lower depths than others. But if you ever were higher on the ladder of Christian experience than you are this morning, to just that extent you are a backslider. Our Lord does not wish us to condemn ourselves for losing that which we never possessed; but to remember from whence, the exact degree of spiritual attainment we once realised, and to compare our present state with it. 'Remember!' – consider it; ponder over it; strive to realise it as the evil and bitter thing it is.

We fear that numbers of Christians reach a fearful degree of backsliding without knowing it. 'Grey hairs are here and there upon Ephraim, yet he knoweth not', and no wonder; they are so occupied with the externals of religion. They are so absorbed in business, or care or pleasure that they have no time to remember. They never stop to compare notes, to observe the landmarks or take the soundings of their spiritual state. They have no time for the old-fashioned duty of self-examination, or if they have, it is so distasteful that they prefer to read, or hear or talk.

Sometimes the Holy Spirit, by some word of God, some sermon or providence, flashes the conviction on their minds that they have lost ground, that they 'have forsaken me, the fountain of living waters, and hewed them out cisterns, broken cisterns, that can hold no water'. But the conviction is painful. They are afraid of the revelation, they shrink from the consequences of its admission even to themselves and, instead of honestly examining into the state of their hearts, they fall back upon their conversion and early experience, and say, 'Surely it must be all right with me, although I have no communion with God, no sensible joy or peace, and but little power over sin. I must be a child of God. Salvation is by faith, not by works; God does not look at me, but at Jesus.'

Instead of remembering from whence they have fallen, they look only to what they have fallen, and try to accommodate the requirements of the word to their miserable experience. Having lost the faith that purifies the heart and manifests its existence by obedience, they try to take refuge in an Antinomian faith, which does neither the one or the other – a faith which makes void the law of God and makes Christ the minister of sin. Thank God, however, they cannot get peace this way! Their countenances belie their creed, and their powerless lives tell to all around that they have only got the shell without the kernel, the form without the power.

If there are any of this class here this morning, my friends, I beseech you your Lord's counsel: remember from whence you have fallen. Reflect on what you once enjoyed. How was it with you in days gone by?

Let me help you to remember by a few practical questions. Did you not once realise a sweet and blessed sense of your acceptance with God, and did not his Spirit witness with your spirit that you were a child of God? And did you not realise that 'there is therefore now no condemnation to them which are in Christ Jesus, who walk not after the flesh, but after the Spirit?' How is it with you now? As you received the Lord Jesus, have you so walked in him that your path has been like that of the just, shining brighter and brighter unto the perfect day, or have you lost your peace, and the joy of the Lord which once was your strength?

Again, did you not once walk in daily communion with God, your prayers being not merely petitions but mediums of sensible intercourse with him? And did not his candle shine brightly on your head? What of your present experience in this respect? Do you still rejoice in this light, or are you groping after him as an absent and far-distant God?

You once realised the power of Christ to rest upon you, so that you were more than conqueror over the world, the flesh and the devil; sin had no more dominion over you; 'old things were passed away', the old spirit of bondage and the helpless misery of a merely convicted state were passed away, and you could sing, 'Thanks be unto God, who giveth us the victory, through Jesus Christ' and 'I can do all things through Christ, which strengtheneth me.'

How is it with you? Do you walk in the liberty wherewith Christ made you free? Or are you gone back to the spirit of bondage again to fear, and to the helplessness of your convicted state, by reason of which you are crying, 'O, wretched man that I am!'? If so, oh, 'remember from whence thou art fallen'.

Your conscience was once tender as the apple of the eye; you eschewed evil and kept as far from its very appearance as you could. You had no fellowship with the godless multitudes who crucified your Lord and trampled underfoot his blessed laws. You kept as far aloof from the world as you might, weeping over its sins, and looking down with pity on its hollow amusements.

What is your present attitude in this matter? Are you still separate from sinners, following the Lamb wheresoever he goeth, or has the daughter of Zion come down from her holy mountain and defiled herself with the abominations of the heathen round about?

You were once full of zeal for the glory of your divine Deliverer, and the salvation of those for whom he died. You could then reprove sin and weep over and expostulate with sinners. You could deny yourself almost your necessary sleep and food in order to promote the interests of your Redeemer's Kingdom. Where is now your zeal for the Lord of hosts? Can you deny self, sacrifice your ease, honour, reputation or wealth for his glory, as you once did? Remember!

Compare your present state with your former one. Let conscience speak, let facts speak, and honestly admit the truth; and if you are condemned, write yourself down as a backslider in heart. You say, 'I do not like the conclusion.' Perhaps not. But if it be true, honesty will be the best policy here, as in everything else. Look the fact in the face, and try to realise its desperate meaning.

I fear too many Christians have far too light an estimate of heart-unfaithfulness. I have sometimes heard them speak of five or 10 years' half-heartedness as a very light thing, slurring it over, as it were, with a very thin and superficial sort of confession; but our Lord does not so regard it. He looks upon it as a very serious matter, a very heinous sin, a most God-dishonouring experience; so much so that he threatens these Ephesian backsliders that unless they repent, notwithstanding all their good works, he will come unto them in judgment and remove their candlestick out of its place.

This is a far greater sin than any you ever committed before you were converted, and you must look at it, reflect on it, remember it, until you have realised its bitterness. Do not be afraid because of the painfulness of the process. Painful operations are often necessary to save life. If you had a bad wound, which required examining and probing, you would not say to the surgeon, 'I cannot bear to look at it; I cannot endure the pain of dressing; cover it up and let it alone.' No, you would know that, painful as would be the process of probing and dressing, it was necessary to save your limb, and perhaps your life; and you would, like a reasonable being, endure the pain, and save your life.

Just so, if you have spiritual wounds they need probing, and perhaps cauterising, before they can be healed; and it is of no use to shrink from the knife of the Great Physician. He knows that it will cause pain; yea, bitter anguish; yet he says, 'Remember!'

Oh, my backsliding friend, bare your heart before him who walks amid the golden candlesticks, and ask him to search it as with a lighted candle. Ask for the realising light of the Holy Spirit to reveal to you your backslidings, and to set your secret sins in the light of his countenance. Ask him to help you to remember by quickening your spiritual perceptions and opening your eyes to see the monstrous ingratitude and cruel infidelity of which you have been guilty.

Instead of refusing to remember, because of the mental suffering involved in the process, methinks we should rejoice to suffer. Seeing that we have wounded our Lord in the house of his friends, we ought to be willing to weep our lives away at the remembrance of our sin, and, if we could, to shed tears of blood as an evidence of our penitence. To have been unfaithful to his saving grace, to have been untrue to his dying love, to have withheld from him that which he purchased with his heart's blood, demands a deeper grief, a more bitter repentance, than that of our unconverted state. May the Lord help those of you who are convicted of this sin to remember, until the fallow ground of your heart is broken up, and your souls cry, 'O, remember not against us former iniquities; let thy tender mercies speedily prevent us, for we are brought very low. Help us, O God of our salvation, and deliver us, and purge away our sins, for thy name's sake.'

The next step is repentance. Now, true repentance implies humiliation, confession and renunciation. When the backslider has remembered until he realises his unfaithfulness in its true heinousness, he will be so deeply humbled that he will be willing to confess his sin before God and his people. I have known Christians deeply convicted of backsliding who were yet too proud to confess it. I have known them cover up their sin, and struggle, and pray, and weep, and labour to get back their peace and power, till they were almost driven to distraction; but I never knew one succeed who refused to make an honest confession. While the backslider in heart is too proud to confess that he is one, the laws of mind, as well as the Word of God, forbid that he should be restored to pardon and peace.

'When I kept silence,' says David, describing such a state, 'my bones waxed old through my roaring all the day long; [then] I said I will confess my transgressions unto the Lord; and thou forgavest the iniquity of my sin.' If we sin against an earthly friend or benefactor, the laws of mind require that, before we can obtain a sense of reconciliation and peace, we must confess the wrong. And all God's requirements and conditions are beautifully adjusted to the laws of our nature; therefore he requires us to confess our sins, and then 'He is faithful and just to forgive us our sins.'

Perhaps someone asks, 'But if I confess to God, is not that enough?' We answer: it depends on the nature of the offence. If it has been against God only, it may be so; but if it has involved or injured others, it must be confessed to them. 'If thou bring thy gift to the altar, and there rememberest that thy brother hath aught against thee, leave there thy gift before the altar, and go thy way; first be reconciled to thy brother, and then come and offer thy gift. … Confess your faults one to another, that ye may be healed.'

Now, the backslider in heart has necessarily influenced and injured others by his coldness, deadness, and inconsistency, and in many cases so deeply that nothing but an honest, straightforward confession on his part can win for the truth any influence over them.

The backsliding Christian falsely represents the religion of Jesus, and indirectly teaches men that it is what he exhibits it to be. Now, on conviction of his unfaithfulness, he is bound in common honesty to redeem his Christianity from the stigma which his inconsistency has brought upon it and to tell those who have witnessed his life that its defects have been attributable not to the religion of Jesus, but to the want of it.

I have sometimes thought, on hearing the professions of the Lord's people, that a little confession would do a great deal more good. There is a mighty power in confession. A thorough and honest confession of backsliding and inconsistency on the part of Christians would do more to convince and arouse the unconverted within their influence than all their professions have done for years gone by, because it would convince the unsaved that they were real and sincere, which at present they do not believe.

Many of you will remember reading a beautiful illustration of what I am saying in the report of the American revival, some seven or eight years ago, respecting a Christian merchant in that country. He does not appear to have been by any means an indifferent professor; on the contrary, he had felt some anxiety about the young men in his employ and had lent them books and invited them to hear earnest ministers, and talked piously to them in a general and indirect sort of way, but all this, as it generally does, had failed to win any of them to Christ, or even to convince them that they were sinners.

One day, as he was walking through the streets reflecting on the failure of all his efforts, he was led, doubtless by the divine Spirit, to see the reason of this failure. He remembered. 'Is it any wonder,' said he to himself, 'that I have failed, seeing how inconsistently I have often acted; what a worldly spirit I have exhibited; what an undue absorption in business; and how little real anxiety I have manifested about the souls of my young men? I never took one of them aside and spoke to him directly and feelingly of his accountability and danger. Oh, how cold and dead and indifferent I have been.'

These reflections so filled him with grief and humiliation that he resolved on taking the first opportunity for confessing his unfaithfulness and speaking pointedly and faithfully to them about their soul. This he did, and in a few weeks the majority of them were blessedly converted to God.

This was the effect of confession. That merchant might have gone on talking good to those young men until now, and no effect would have been produced. While his practice was so far below his profession, all his direct efforts were neutralised, and thus it is with thousands of professing Christians. They are not altogether indifferent about others, they try to do a little for the Lord, but their endeavours are all lost because of their half-heartedness and inconsistency.

If there are any here who feel this to be true in their case, my dear friends, let me urge you to follow the example of the merchant. Remember your unfaithfulness, till you are sufficiently humbled to be willing to confess it to those whom you have injured by it. This is just what is needful, and all that is needful in many an instance where Christians have been praying for years for unconverted relatives and friends.

Suppose, a Christian wife here this morning, you have an unconverted husband for whom you have been praying for many years but you are conscious that he has witnessed much in your conduct and spirit which has been at variance with the Christianity which you have professed. Now, this discrepancy between your practice and profession lies like an enemy in ambush against all extraneous efforts to bring saving truth to bear on the conscience of your husband, and no doubt an honest confession on your part would do more to break his heart and win him to the Saviour than all the sermons he has heard for years gone by.

If you are in doubt, try it. If you are convicted of backsliding, go home, and with meekness and tears of bitter penitence tell your husband so. Tell him that the Spirit has convinced you of your half-heartedness and inconsistency. Tell him that you are ashamed of the past, and resolved by God's grace to lead a new life. Put your arm round his neck and ask him to join you. Then get on your knees and pour out your soul in confession to God, and see whether your husband's heart will not be moved, and admittance gained for the truth and Spirit of God. And vice-versa, let the husband do so with his wife. I tell you that your confession will do more than all your professions have ever done.

And just so in the case of Christian parents who have lived in a half-hearted state before their children. Oh, how much has been said and written as to the reasons why so few comparatively of the children of Christians get converted in early life. I think the answer could be given, and the mystery explained in one word: unfaithfulness. How can parents expect to win their children to Christ if they constantly exhibit an un-Christlike spirit, and trample under foot the plainest teachings of his Word?

How frequently the children of professing parents seem to entertain a greater malignity against the religion of Jesus than do the children of thorough worldlings, and no wonder, seeing that the very name of Christianity has been made to stink in their nostrils by the inconsistency of the parents. They are taught in precept that they are to be sincere, truthful, unselfish, unworldly, but they see in practice the constant exhibition of principles directly contrary; and hence they learn to despise both their parents and the religion which they profess. If there are any inconsistent parents here this morning, my friends, if you desire the conversion of your children, go home and take down the barriers which your unfaithfulness has raised in their hearts against the reception of the gospel. Go and confess to your children, or if their youth renders this inexpedient, gather them around the family altar, and confess it all to God in their presence. Make a fresh and full dedication of yourselves, of your children, of your all to him, beseeching him with strong cries and tears to give you grace to live wholly for him. Do this with godly sincerity, your own hearts being truly broken up, and no matter how careless or ungracious your children may have been, you will find them melted into tenderness, and in all probability convinced of sin.

So greatly does God delight in honesty of heart in his people that he never fails to give the accompanying power of the Spirit to those who exercise it. I have not a doubt that an honest confession of backsliding on the part of all unfaithful ministers would open the windows of Heaven and bring down such a flood of grace on their barren and worldly churches as would shake our land from end to end.

I remember reading a very striking and affecting illustration of this some years ago, in connection with the experience of a dear man of God who, during the early years of his Christian career, had been a man of extraordinary devotedness, zeal, and self-sacrifice, but gradually and almost imperceptibly to himself he had fallen from his first love. Though still abounding in good works, and looked up to by all as a pattern of piety, he had lost the power which once characterised him. The Lord showed him from whence he had fallen in a very simple and effective manner, by bringing him into close contact with a man filled with the Spirit and burning with zeal for the salvation of souls, thus by the law of contrast flashing on him the conviction that he had lost his first love.

The backslider in heart began to 'remember'. He said to himself, 'I was once like that man. I felt as he does; I rejoiced as he does; I prayed as he does; I laboured as be does. But I am not like him now. Oh, my God, I am a backslider in heart.'

The discovery almost overwhelmed him. He realised its bitterness and agonised over its consequences, until his distress reached a climax and, kneeling down, he prayed in an agony, telling the Lord that if he would restore him to his first love he would confess his heart-backsliding to his brethren and do all in his power to counteract the evil effects of his former coldness and unfaithfulness.

I need not say that the Lord heard and answered. This was all he wanted of his servant, in order to do his pouring in the oil and wine of his love and consolation. Like the disciples on the day of Pentecost, he rose from his knees filled with the Spirit. The next day there was an official meeting, in which he had to take part. At the appointed time some dozen of the leading men assembled. After the business was gone through, he asked to be allowed to make a few remarks and then, with the simplicity of a little child, like an honest-hearted man as he was, he related the experience of the last few days.

He confessed to his brethren his heart-backsliding, told them how the Lord had convinced him of it, and how graciously he had restored him to his first love. The brethren present were melted into tears. They sobbed and cried like children and, when he had done, broke out into a general confession of backsliding and unfaithfulness. They continued in the deepest humiliation of soul, confessing and bewailing their sins until midnight.

As one after another poured out his soul in confession and supplication, the Holy Ghost fell on them, and there commenced in that room on that memorable night a revival which swept hundreds into the Church of Christ, many of whom are now in Heaven. All this was brought about by the power of confession. That man might have preached on until the end of his days and never have done one tithe of the good which this one open, honest confession did.

Oh, what a deal of praying there is for revivals, and for spiritual visitations, which is sheer hypocrisy! The Church might have a revival as wide and deep and powerful as she asks, if she would only comply with the conditions on which God can grant it – if she would remember her unfaithfulness, honestly confess and forsake her sins, and bring into God's storehouse the tithes of which she is so flagrantly robbing him. But it is easier to utter vain repetitions and leave the responsibility of the damnation of souls upon God than for Christians to humble themselves, confess before the world their fallen and powerless condition and pay their vows unto the Lord.

The Lord only wants a wholehearted faithful people and the walls of many a Jericho would fall, and a nation be born in a day. Oh, may the Lord send upon his backsliding Israel the spirit of conviction and of mourning! May he open her eyes to see from whence she has fallen, and enable her to repent, to come down into the dust and cry, 'Unclean, unclean!' until her iniquity is purged, her backslidings healed and her lips touched with living fire from off his pure and holy altar.

But, further, repentance not only implies humiliation and confession, but renunciation, sometimes the hardest of all. 'Put away the evil of your doings' is an indispensable condition of restoration to the favour and peace of God. Christ Jesus came to save his people from their sins, not in them, and those who will not be saved from their sins prove beyond a question that they are none of his.

I have known many professing Christians try hard to get peace while holding on to some sin, or allowing some idol, but I never knew one succeed. You may preach faith for ever to a soul thus temporising with evil, but its consciousness will be too strong for your theories. You must show that soul that it can never believe till it is willing to part with evil. Not that it must save itself, but that it must be willing to be saved from sin.

This was the principle on which Christ dealt with the young ruler, and which is insisted on again and again by Christ and his apostles. I am satisfied that thousands of professing Christians are kept in bondage and darkness through not understanding this fundamental principle of the economy of salvation. They hear so much about faith, and so little about the conditions of faith, that they get bewildered, and instead of repenting and putting away the evil, that their sins may be blotted out, they spend all their time in trying to work themselves up into a faith as unphilosophical as it is unscriptural. Consequently, they fail to get peace, and live in perpetual condemnation and misery. So it must ever be with those who ignore God's way and take their own.

I remember a striking illustration of this, in connection with some services I held in a distant part of the country. A gentleman called on me and sent in to ask if I would see him without an introduction, as he did not wish to reveal his name. I said, 'Oh, certainly; if I could be of any service to him, I did not wish to know who he was.' Accordingly, he came in and told me his story.

He said that he had been attending my Thursday morning meetings for believers, and he thought perhaps I could help him as he was in a most difficult and painful position. I found that he had once lived very near to God and known much of his grace and love, but in a time of partial backsliding he had been induced to enter into partnership in business with an unconverted man. His partner, though a respectable, moral man, after the standard of the world, practised and allowed things in the management of the business which my visitor's conscience condemned. 'And though,' said he, 'I protest against them, and have no share in their preparation, yet I share in the profits of the business, and my name goes forth to the public as responsible for all that is done, and I feel condemned on account of it.'

He told me that he had lost his peace and had tried in every way to regain it. He had fasted and prayed, and wept and struggled, till his body was quite worn. He had been to seek the advice of every minister for miles around, and had sought the counsels and prayers of his Christian friends, in vain. 'What am I to do?' said he. 'I have considerable capital invested. My friends are very anxious that I should get on, and others are involved in my success.'

I felt the importance of the case and truly sympathised with the young man, but to me his path seemed plain as daylight.

I looked up for a word that should convince him, and then said, 'Well, my dear sir, I can only say that, for myself, I should as soon expect the favour of God in hell, as on earth, while I was doing or allowing anything for which my conscience condemned me.'

The arrow went home. He said, 'I see, I see. I shall have to come out at all costs.' I said, 'I believe you will.' And then I tried to show him how much richer he would be with an approving conscience and the smile of God – even in poverty, if the Lord should so will – than with wealth and affluence in his present wretched state of mind.

I afterwards learnt who he was, and was most thankful to find that he had followed the light and given up the ungodly alliance. Now, I say, this young man might have wept himself into the grave and never have regained his peace unless he had renounced his sin. It was utterly useless telling him to exercise faith for deliverance. It was as impossible for him to believe as it was for him to fly while he was maintaining this controversy with his conscience and with the Spirit. He must first put away the evil and then it was easy to believe.

Another case illustrative of what I have been saying occurred in connection with my labours in the North of England. The gentleman in whose house I was staying said to me, one morning, on our return from the chapel, 'Do you know what I have done? I have thrown my pipe and cigars and tobacco-box on to the dunghill and I have made up my mind to smoke no more.'

He then said that he had waged a controversy with his conscience and with the Spirit of God for 15 years about this paltry gratification, living in a state of perpetual condemnation and sacrificing the power and usefulness which he had once realised for the sake of this idol. Immediately on putting away the indulgence, peace was restored to his soul and he began to labour for the Lord as in days gone by.

I could give numbers of similar illustrations but these will suffice to show you that it matters not whether the controverted practice involves the loss of hundreds of pounds, or only of a pipe of tobacco. It is not the greatness or smallness of the matter in itself, but the principle of obedience which is involved in the controversy. While there is a vestige of insubordination to the requirements of conscience and of God, there can be no peace.

On this point, thousands of professing Christians mistake. They allow themselves in things which they feel to be unlawful and then strive and pray to obtain a sense of acceptance through Christ. They want the Spirit to witness with their spirits that their ways please God, while they know that their ways are such as cannot please him. Therefore they want the Spirit to witness to a lie, which is impossible.

No, my backsliding friend, there is but one way back to peace and joy and usefulness, and that is your Lord's own way, which always implies forsaking sin, putting away the evil. Christ Jesus is too much in love with his Father's will to dwell with those who will not obey it. The unalterable condition of his presence and his smile is doing the will of his Father.

The 'sons of God are led by the Spirit of God' and if you refuse to be thus led you cannot have the spirit of adoption. Do you see this? Do you feel it? If so, will you put away those sins and iniquities which have separated you from your God? Will you let your idols go, and now for ever renounce all that is contrary to his holy will? If you will, you will find it easy to take the next step in your Lord's way of restoration; nay, you will come with gladness to do 'your first works'.

I think the Lord has enabled me to show you that restoration to first love is impossible without the renunciation of evil; so I think, by the aid of the Blessed Spirit, I shall be able to show that it is equally impossible without consecration to known duty. I have known backsliders in heart who have 'remembered' till their hearts have been well-nigh broken, and who, I believe, have honestly put away the occasions of their backsliding, who have nevertheless shrunk from embracing the Cross in the form of some suffering or duty to which the Spirit has called them, and thus have found it impossible to exercise the faith necessary to their healing.

I once knew a widow lady who, though she tried every method, and that for a long time, to regain her peace, could not, because she refused to conduct family prayers, to which duty the Spirit of God urged her. I have known others who have felt that they ought to confess their backsliding state, and they have tried anything and everything else in vain, but immediately on confessing have obtained a sense of acceptance.

I know a lady who maintained a controversy with the Spirit for four years, about giving up her husband to a work to which she believed God had called him, but which involved much sacrifice and trial. Many a time she said, with anguish of spirit, 'Anything but this, Lord!' but this was the very thing which the Lord required, and not until, like Abraham, she gave up the best beloved of her soul to the will of God did she recover her peace and joy.

I am acquainted with a minister who, after trying for a long time to lead a deeply convicted sinner into faith, paused and said, 'Excuse me, madam, but I think there is something that you are not willing to give up, or to do.' After a few minutes' silence she burst out weeping afresh and, after a terrible struggle, said, 'Oh, I cannot forgive the murderer of my husband.' Surely if any compromise in the conditions of salvation were possible in any case, it was in this. But no. The Spirit of God had already shown that lady what hindered her reception of Christ, and, instead of urging her to believe, that minister, as a wise co-worker with the Spirit, told her that, difficult as the duty might appear, she must embrace it and forgive the man who had so deeply injured her.

She made the effort – that is, her will submitted – and immediately the Spirit helped her infirmities, and enabled her fully and freely to forgive. Almost at the same moment she was enabled to believe unto salvation.

I might give you numbers of similar cases which have come under my own observation but I trust these will be sufficient to show what I mean by consecration as a condition of faith. I think I may say, without exaggeration, that I have conversed with hundreds of backsliders of different degrees, and I never knew one restored to first love who refused compliance with known duty. 'To him who knoweth to do good and doeth it not, to him it is sin', and in wilful sin there is no salvation.

Do you see this, my dear friends, you who are mourning an absent God? Are you willing to consecrate yourselves this day unto the Lord? Do you honestly renounce those things through which you have lost your peace, and brought leanness into your souls? Do you embrace the will, the whole will of God, as your rule of life? Will you bring into his storehouse the tithes of a wholehearted service and a cheerful obedience? In short, will you give him that which he claims – yourself and your all? If so, his word to you is, 'I will heal your backslidings, I will love you freely; for mine anger is turned away from you. … I will betroth thee unto me for ever; yea, I will betroth thee unto me in righteousness, and in judgment, and in loving-kindness, and in mercies. I will even betroth thee unto me in faithfulness, and thou shalt know the Lord.'

Satan tempts you to shrink from a full consecration for fear you should not be able to live up to it; but if you will comply with the conditions, God will fulfil this promise. If you will only yield yourself up without reserve, he will work in you to will and to do of his good pleasure.

Hear your Lord's Word: 'If a man love me, he will keep my words; and my Father will love him, and we will come unto him, and make our abode with him.' Surely, with the Father and Son, you will be able to do and suffer all things. The reason for your past failures has been the want of God. When God comes to dwell in you, when he betroths you to him in faithfulness for ever, you will fail no more. His strength will be made perfect in your weakness; you will be able to do all things through Christ, who strengtheneth you.

I doubt not some of you are saying, 'How shall I realise the fulfilment of these blessed promises?' I answer: by simple faith. Just as you trusted at first for justification and rested not on your feelings but on his promises, so now you must cast yourself on his blessed assurances of healing and of strength. Having the testimony of your own spirit that you comply with the conditions, in putting away the evil and embracing the will of God, you have nothing to do but to throw yourself on his bosom and rest in his love. The mercy seat is sprinkled with the blood of an all-sufficient atonement, so that he can receive and pardon even backsliders, if they will only believe. He says, 'Return unto me and I will heal your backslidings.'

Now you do return, will you not believe that he heals you? He says he will. Dare you make him a liar? You have no alternative. If you come, he either does, or does not receive you. He says he does. Oh, believe him, and he will betroth you unto him in faithfulness for ever.

Four

Dealing with anxious souls – an address to Christian workers

I have long desired to say a few words on the subject of dealing with the anxious. It seems to me that if there is one work in the vineyard more important than another it is that of guiding souls in this the most momentous crisis of their being. A mistake here will probably prove a fatal mistake, blighting all the joy and strength of future life.

I fear thousands have been mistaken here. Mere impression has been mistaken for conviction, and an intellectual faith for saving faith of the heart, hence so much of the spurious Christianity prevalent amongst us.

We should be very careful, in all our dealings with anxious souls, first to find out their exact position with regard to sin. In all spiritual awakenings there are always numbers of individuals who are partially awakened and sufficiently impressed to become anxious, like the young ruler and Agrippa, but who, like them, are not sufficiently so to be willing to give up their sins.

Such individuals frequently present themselves as penitents desiring to be saved, and too often those who have to deal with them, instead of finding out their true state and working together with the Holy Ghost to deepen conviction and drive them up to real submission to God, begin at once to talk of Christ having paid their debt and done everything for them, so that they have nothing to do but to believe and they are saved.

Now it seems to me that to prevent such a grievous mistake, with all its bitter consequences, everyone who deals with souls should have a clear and definite understanding of the conditions on which alone God pardons and receives repenting sinners. These conditions always have been, and ever must remain, the same, seeing that the principles of the divine government can never change. Hence we find that, alike under the old and new dispensations, God's unalterable condition of pardon is the forsaking of evil.

'Let the wicked forsake his way, and the unrighteous man his thoughts: and let him return unto the Lord, and he will have mercy upon him: and to our God, for he will abundantly pardon. … Turn ye, turn ye, from your evil ways; for why will ye die, O house of Israel. … Have I any pleasure at all that the wicked should die? saith the Lord God; and not that he should return from his ways and live?'

Of course the wicked were to return in the appointed way of sacrifice and offering, but the condition of the acceptance of the offering, and the pardon of the transgressor, was the forsaking of evil. Just so now: the sinner must return to God by the new and living way, the 'sacrifice once offered', but the condition of his acceptance through this sacrifice is the forsaking of evil. Unless he is willing to let go his sins and be separated from his idols, the sacrifice of Christ will avail him nothing but to increase his condemnation tenfold.

It seems astounding that, with the Bible in their hands, so many professing to be guides of souls should mistake here, and, oh, it makes one's heart bleed to think of the consequences. We have thousands self-deceived, counting themselves believers, who never knew the pangs of real repentance, whose hearts never really turned from sin to righteousness, from Satan to God, who suppose they have been converted, but who have manifestly never been regenerated, who live as the slaves and votaries of the world while they profess to be children of God. In short, who regard themselves as Christians while they are still in the gall of bitterness and in the bond of iniquity.

Let us mind not to be partakers of other men's sins in this matter. Let us settle in our minds that there can be no conversion without conviction of sin, and such conviction as makes the soul willing to abandon evil. Casting ourselves on the Spirit for the necessary tenderness in doing it, let us not be afraid to probe the wounds with which every unregenerate soul is covered, and above all things let us avoid giving false comfort and pressing the inquirer into a mere intellectual faith, while he is cleaving to idols. Let us ever remember that saving faith is impossible while the soul's desires are set on that which is evil. It must be so awakened and convicted as to turn its face towards God, and so intensely desire his favour and love as to be willing to give up all evil as a condition of attaining it.

I repeat, it is astounding that, with the Bible in their hands, some teachers can so confound things that differ, and so wrongly 'divide the word of truth' as to make 'Christ the minister of sin', by preaching 'only believe' to people who are holding on to sin. You will hear some of these good people asserting that we have nothing to do with conditions now, that repentance is not necessary to faith. 'Only believe and you shall be saved … Jesus did it all, long, long ago.'

Truly! But what was it Jesus did? His own work, not mine. He lived, laboured, wept, suffered and died and atoned for me, and he did it all till he cried, 'It is finished'; but I nowhere read that he 'repented' and 'turned to God', and did 'works meet for repentance', and 'believed' and 'obeyed the gospel' for me. This he commands every soul to do for itself, or perish.

The only way in which Jesus is represented as saving men is in 'turning them away from their iniquities', and until a soul is willing to let him save it from sin, he cannot save it at all. Let us always try to find out whether inquirers are willing or desire to be saved from evil, and are coming to Christ for this end, or whether they are only desirous of being saved from hell, and consequently holding on to sin. Here is just the difference between the true and spurious repentance, and on this hinges the result whether we shall bring into the Church another mere professor, a Simon Magus, or one who will follow Christ in the regeneration of the spirit, having his heart purified by a living faith.

'Oh,' but say some, 'what did Paul say to the jailor? He did not say anything about conditions or repentance, but simply, "Believe ...". I answer we do not know all that Paul said on this occasion, for in the next verse we read that 'they [Paul and Silas] spake unto him the Word of the Lord, and to all his house'. Mark, this was before his profession of faith and baptism!

Now who can tell how much this Word of the Lord implied? Doubtless the apostle explained on this, as on other occasions, what constituted that 'obedience to the truth' through which the jailor, in common with all other penitents, was to be purified. But, supposing that the apostle had spoken no other words than 'Believe on the Lord Jesus Christ', this would only prove that in this particular instance no other counsel was necessary, because the jailor was prepared for it.

He had come to the point of full submission where saving faith first becomes possible. The whole tenor of the narrative shows that the jailor was a fully awakened, truly repenting, deeply humbled sinner, ready to do anything. 'He sprang in, and came trembling, and fell down before Paul and Silas, and brought them out, and said, "Sirs, what must I do to be saved?"'

Observe, 'He brought them out.' He began immediately to bring forth fruits meet for repentance. The earthquake had torn the bandages from his eyes, and the Spirit, through its instrumentality, had shaken his guilty soul and made him realise his danger in the hands of a God who could avenge the wrongs of his people after such a fashion.

He was so deeply convicted, so fully turned round 'from darkness to light', that he was ready to do anything. He was not ashamed to confess his wickedness, to kneel before his prisoners and plead with them to show him what to do. And if Paul had told him, as Jesus did the young ruler, to sell his goods and give to the poor, there cannot be a doubt but he would have embraced the command at once, as Zacchæus did the obligation to make restitution. The intense earnestness of his gesture and question shows that he was willing to be saved at any; ready to do anything; and, therefore, nothing more remained to be done but to believe.

Now, wherever we find a soul in this attitude, be it our highest privilege – our chief joy – to point him to the Lamb of God, and to show him the way of faith more perfectly. But, oh! let us mind not to do it (except as a motive to submission) until this attitude is attained. Let us beware of a theoretical or sentimental faith, which leaves the heart unwashed, unrenewed, unsanctified. It is just here that thousands get the faith of devils, which is like the body without the spirit – dead! From this bitter root springs nearly all the Antinomianism of this age. With this untempered slime of the old serpent, half the superstructure of the professing Church is joined together. Let us spurn it and warn souls against it.

Let us mind the order of God in our dealing with souls. He made them and he knows best how to dissect them. It seems astonishing that any difference of view can have obtained on the point with passages so direct, full, and relevant as Acts 26:18, 20. Surely our glorified Lord understood the constitution of the human soul and knew best as to the method or order in which his truth and spirit operate upon it.

There are two or three considerations which give this passage special weight. It comes from the lips of our risen Lord. It was given after the gospel dispensation was opened in all its fulness. It was given to Paul, the principal expounder of the doctrine of justification by faith, and therefore his views of faith could not have been contradictory to its teaching.

It was applied alike to Jews and Gentiles. 'To open their eyes' – to awaken and make them realise their danger as sinners – 'and to turn them from darkness to light'. That is, from the choice or embrace of evil, to the choice or embrace of righteousness, and 'from the power of Satan unto God'. That is, from being committed to the power of Satan to committal to the power of God: 'That they may receive forgiveness of sins and inheritance among them which are sanctified by faith that is in me.'

Observe here what a deal has to be done in the soul before it can receive forgiveness of sins. Its eyes must be opened. To what? Its own sinfulness and danger and misery. Then, under the sight of this, it must be turned right round from the embrace or desire of evil to the embrace or desire of righteousness (though yet powerless to do, it must choose and desire righteousness).

The attitude of the will must change with respect to evil and good. It must turn round from the one to the other in purpose and desire. Then 'it must be turned from committal to the power of Satan unto God'. It must abjure Satan as its rightful sovereign, and at least will to put itself under the power of God. And all this in order that it may receive forgiveness of sin. This is made an absolute condition of its receiving forgiveness.

Now, I maintain that this is the only possible interpretation of this important text, not only of our version but of the original in all its purity; and if so, what becomes of the theory that there are no conditions, and that repentance and forsaking of evil and choosing good is not necessary to saving faith? Further, we see in the 18th verse how literally Paul understood, and how implicitly he followed, this divine order, for in verse 20 he says he 'showed first unto them of Damascus, and at Jerusalem, and throughout all the coasts of Judæa, and then to the Gentiles that they should repent and turn to God, and do works meet for repentance'.

Now, certainly Paul knew what he preached, and there could not be any contradiction in his mind between these necessary conditions of faith, and faith itself. Therefore, when he speaks of faith only being necessary to a sinner's justification, he must always assume that these conditions are complied with, otherwise he contradicts himself and sets aside the order of this divine commission.

I know that Paul teaches that faith alone is the hand that takes hold of Christ, but of course he assumes that the feet of repentance and submission have brought the soul near enough for this hand to reach him; in other words, that, by the Spirit's power, he is so convinced of sin, of righteousness and of judgment as to be willing to forsake every evil way and to flee for refuge to the hope set before him.

It seems difficult to imagine how any idea of pardon and reconciliation can have obtained in the Church which does not presuppose these conditions, seeing that Jesus laid it down again and again as a fundamental principle that no man could become his disciple, or follow him, till he was willing to renounce every thing, and every being, antagonistic to his supreme love and dominion in the soul (Luke 14:26, 30; Matthew 5:29, 30; 10:37).

We find also that the apostles invariably acted on the assumption that until the soul turned round from evil to God it could not believe (Acts 24:25). I would ask, 'Why did not Paul press Felix to believe on the Lord Jesus? He trembled, as did the jailor.'

The reason is evident: he did not submit to God and forsake sin (Acts 8:22, 23; Acts 20:21; Luke 24:47; Acts 5:31; Romans 1:18; Romans 2:3-10). The principle laid down in these texts is recognised by Jesus in his messages to the seven churches: there is no promise of pardon, even to backsliders, without such repentance as leads to the putting away of evil. This, then, is the test of genuine repentance: willingness to put away sin. Until this is attained, let us not dare to attempt to comfort any soul, for in so doing we shall not be workers together with God, but the tools of Satan, doing exactly what he desires to be done.

My dear friends, ponder on these suggestions. They will bear examination. Carefully compare Scripture with Scripture on this point, seeking the light of the Holy Spirit, and you will be saved from healing the health of the Lord's people slightly; from increasing the number of those who have a form of godliness without the power.

The next important step in dealing with anxious souls is to present to them the proper object of faith, which is Christ Jesus himself, and not merely the divine testimony concerning him. There is a vast difference between these two objects of faith. The one ends with the intellect, the other purifies the heart. That method of leading souls into faith which presents the truth as a system, or declaration, on the reception or belief of which the soul is to reckon itself saved, fails to bring the soul into contact with a living personal Christ, and possesses no living principle by which to graft it into the vine as a living branch. Truly the divine testimony concerning Christ must be received and believed; but this is not to be the ultimate object of faith, but only the medium through which the soul's trust is to be transferred to the living person testified of.

Here arises another fatal error of this day, through which, I fear, numbers never realise any other God than the Bible, or any other Saviour than a powerless, intellectual belief in the letter of it. They believe the truth about Christ, about his life and death, his sacrifice and intercession. They believe, as enquirers often tell me they do, that Jesus died for them and that he intercedes for them, but they do not believe that his sacrifice actually satisfies the Father for their sins, or that his intercession so far prevails with God for them that he does now actually pardon and receive them because of it. If they believe this, of course their anxiety would immediately cease and they would begin to sing the new song of praise and thanksgiving.

The mind is too often occupied with the theory of divine truth instead of the living person whom the truth sets forth. Now it seems clear to me that the divine testimony concerning Christ may be believed, and frequently is believed, without their existing a particle of saving trust in him as a personal Saviour. Here is the secret of so many apparently believing and devout people living in systematic disobedience to God. Their minds are convinced of the truth, and their emotions are frequently stirred by it, but they have no life, no spiritual power in them by which to resist temptation or live above the world, because their faith does not embrace a living Saviour able to save them to the uttermost, but only the truth about him.

Take an illustration. Suppose you are sick almost unto death. A friend brings you a testimony concerning some wonderful physician who has cured many such cases, and is fully able and willing to undertake yours. Now, you may receive the record of your friend concerning the skill and success of this physician's treatment, and you may fully believe it, and yet there may be some reason why you shrink from putting yourself into his hands and trusting him with your life. You may believe all that is said about him, and yet fail so to trust in his person as to give yourself up fully into his power. Just so there are numbers who believe God's testimony concerning his Son, that Jesus has atoned for their sin, and that his treatment would cure them of its disease, who do not trust him to do it for them, no, not for a single moment. Here is the difference between a dead and a living faith; between a faith that lies useless on the shelves of the intellect, or bubbles up on the waves of mere emotion, and that which renews the soul in righteousness, and makes it the abode of an indwelling Christ.

The term faith is used in several different senses in the Scripture, but when used to designate that act through which the soul is justified before God, and renewed by his Spirit, it always signifies trust in, or committal to a living Saviour. The word used to signify this trust is sometimes rendered 'commit', as in John 2:24: 'But Jesus did not commit himself unto them, because he knew all men.' He did not believe in them, or trust them with his person. He did not commit himself into their power. This is just what God requires the sinner to do in order to be saved: to commit himself to the faithfulness and power of Jesus. Again, we have the same word in Luke 16:11: 'If therefore ye have not been faithful in the unrighteous mammon, who will commit to your trust the true riches?'

Now, it is evident that the scriptural idea of saving faith is that of the absolute committal of the whole being over to the faithfulness and power of

93

Jesus, and not merely a belief, however firm, of the records of certain facts concerning him. I may believe that he is the Saviour; that he died for me; that he intercedes for me; that he has promised to save me, as thousands do; and yet I may have no trust in him as now doing all this for me, and consequently draw no sap, no spiritual virtue, from him.

Saving faith consists in a firm trust in the person of Jesus, and committal of the soul to him by an unwavering act of confidence in him for all that the Bible presents him to be, as the Redeemer and Saviour of men: 'For I know whom I have believed, and am persuaded that he is able to keep that which I have committed unto him against that day' (2 Timothy 1:12). And as soon as this trust is exercised, the testimony of the Spirit is given to adoption and the soul knows that it has passed from death unto life.

Of course this trust is exercised through the testimony of God to his Son, but the Son is the object of trust, and not the testimony merely. This is most important to bear in mind in our efforts to lead souls into saving faith.

And now it becomes a question of deepest interest how best to lead true penitent sinners to exercise this trust. The first thing generally to be done is to present Jesus as willing to meet the realised desperateness of the sinner's case, as every true penitent thinks himself the chief of sinners, and his own a peculiarly bad case. We should try to show him that the question of salvation does not hinge on the greatness or smallness of a sinner's guilt but on the fact of his accepting Jesus as a sufficient atonement for it. We should try to show him how almost all the instances of conversion recorded in the Bible were great sinners, and how Jesus came to seek that which was absolutely lost, and how the depths of his love can only be shown on very bad cases.

When we have succeeded in leading the soul to apprehend the sufficiency of the atonement to cover, and the willingness of Jesus to pardon the past, unbelief will generally fasten on the future, and the inquirer will say, 'Ah! but if I were forgiven, I should fall again into sin.'

Now is the time to bring the soul face to face with a personal, living Saviour. We must present Christ's ability to save to the uttermost – of the soul's need and circumstances – all them who come unto God by him. We must get the soul's eye fixed on Jesus, not only as a sacrifice but as a Saviour, a Deliverer, an Almighty Friend, who has promised to dwell and abide with the believer, delivering him out of the hands of all his enemies. We should not give up till, by the help of the Spirit, we can lead the soul to expect in Jesus the supply of all its needs. When this is accomplished, we should lead the soul on to claim this Saviour now.

When arrived at this point I have sometimes found it very helpful to ask, 'Well, now, when did

Jesus pardon and receive the penitents who came to him in the days of his flesh?' Waiting for an answer, thus compelling the mind's attention to the point, the inquirer will generally say, 'I suppose when they came to him.'

I reply, 'Of course that was the only time to receive them: when they came, not an hour before or an hour after, but at the moment they came, and it is the same now. He receives returning sinners when they come.'

Now, you come, confessing and forsaking all your sins, and willing to follow him wherever he may lead you. Does he receive you? He said he would in no wise cast you out if you came. Does he cast you out?

The penitent will generally say, 'No, I trust not.' Then what does he? He must either take you in or cast you out just now, because you come just now. Which is it?

Sometimes we get the answer, 'I hope he takes me in.' Then we try to show that this is not the place for hope. Only to hope that Jesus means what he says is to insult him and drive him away. You must trust him and believe now that he takes you in.

Oh, what struggles I have often witnessed just at this point! Satan understands the power of this committal, and withstands it with all his subtlety and malice. But if we are firm, and armed with the power of the Spirit, and persistently and relentlessly press the soul up to present trust, the result is certain. Condemnation is taken away, light breaks on the soul, and the new song bursts spontaneously from the lips, even praise and thanksgiving to our God.

In some cases it requires no little sympathy, tact and firmness to meet the wiles of unbelief and the stratagems of Satan, even in dealing with very sincere and truly submissive souls. Fear of being deceived is generally one of the greatest difficulties. In such cases it is well to explain to the penitent that there is no ground for this fear, seeing that this way of salvation is of God's own appointing, and that, although it seems an easy way to be saved, after living so long in sin and rebellion the ease of it is all on the sinner's side, and not on the side of the Saviour. We should explain at what a terrible cost of sacrifice and suffering to the Son of God this simple, easy way was opened, and how ungrateful it is to put it away, as if it were too good to be true, because God has made it so simple.

It is well to encourage the inquirer to trust by reminding him that every truly saved soul on earth, and every redeemed spirit in Heaven, was saved in this way: by simple faith alone. It is often very helpful to get the penitent to use the language of faith with his lips, even before his heart can fully go with it. I have seen many a one rise into faith while repeating after me the text, rendered in the first person, 'He was wounded for my transgressions' or 'Thou hast said, him that cometh to thee thou wilt in no wise cast out. Lord, I come; thou dost not cast me out; thou takest me in' or 'Tis done; the great transaction done; I am my Lord's and he is mine' or 'I can believe, I do believe, that Jesus saves me now', repeating such passages or stanzas over and over again till the heart follows the tongue and the venture is made.

Of course we cannot give counsels for every individual case. There are great diversities in the temperaments and circumstances of different individuals requiring a wise adaption of treatment at the moment for which the Spirit alone can endow us. Let us, however, only be clear and faithful on the two momentous points of a true and thorough repentance and an intelligent and implicit trust in a living Saviour, and every minor question will easily be met, and the souls whom the Lord shall honour us to bring into his family will not be stillborn ghosts of a sinewless sentimentalism but strong, hardy, cross-bearing, Christ-honouring, soul-winning men and women, able to open Heaven and shake hell by their faith and zeal and effort in our Redeemer's Kingdom.

Five

Compel them to come in

ON a certain Sabbath, some years ago, I was passing down a narrow, thickly-populated street on my way to hear a much-honoured minister of Christ, anticipating an evening's enjoyment for myself and hoping to see some anxious ones brought into the Kingdom, when I chanced to look up at the thick rows of small windows above me, where numbers of women were sitting, peering through at the passers-by or listlessly gossiping with each other. It was suggested to my mind with great power, 'Would you not be doing God more service, and acting more like your Redeemer, by turning into some of these houses, speaking to these care-less sinners, and inviting them to the service, than by going to enjoy it yourself?'

I was startled. It was a new thought, and while I was reasoning about it the same inaudible interrogator demanded: 'What effort do Christians put forth, answerable to the command, "Compel them to come in, that my house may be filled"?'

This was accompanied with a light and unction which I knew to be divine. I felt greatly agitated. I felt very guilty. I knew that I had never thus laboured to bring lost sinners to Christ, and, trembling with a sense of my utter weakness, I stood still for a moment, looked up to Heaven, and said, 'Lord, if thou wilt help me, I will try' and without stopping longer to confer with flesh and blood, turned back and commenced my work.

I spoke first to a group of women sitting on a doorstep, and, oh!, what that effort cost me, words cannot describe. But the Spirit helped my infirmities and secured for me a patient and respectful hearing with a promise from some of them to attend the house of God. This much encouraged me. I began to taste the joy which lies hidden under the cross and to realise, in some faint degree, that it is more blessed to give than to receive.

With this timely, loving cordial from my blessed Master I went on to the next group, standing at the entrance of a low, dirty court. Here, again, I was received kindly, and promises were given – no rude repulse, no bitter ridicule, was allowed to shake my new-found confidence or chill my feeble zeal. I began to realise that my Master's feet were behind me; nay, before me, smoothing my path and preparing my way.

This blessed assurance so increased my courage and enkindled my hope, that I ventured to knock at the door of the next house, and when it was opened, to go in and speak to the inmates of Jesus, death, judgment and eternity. The man, who appeared to be one of the better class of mechanics, seemed to be much interested and affected by my words, and promised with his wife to attend the revival services which were being held at the chapel farther on.

With a heart full of gratitude and eyes full of tears I was thinking where I should go next when I observed a woman standing on an adjoining doorstep, with a jug in her hand. My divine Teacher said, 'Speak to that woman.' Satan suggested, 'Perhaps she is intoxicated' but, after a momentary struggle, I introduced myself to her by saying, 'Are the people out who live on this floor?', observing that the lower part of the house was closed.

'Yes,' she said, 'they are gone to chapel', and I thought I perceived a weary sadness in her voice and manner. I said, 'Oh, I am so glad to hear that: how is it that you are not gone to a place of worship?'

'Me?', she said, looking down upon her forlorn appearance, 'I can't go to chapel; I am kept at home by a drunken husband. I have to stop with him to keep him from the public-house, and I have just been fetching him some drink.'

I expressed my sorrow for her and asked if I might come in and see her husband. 'No,' she said, 'he is drunk; you could do nothing with him now.'

I replied, 'I do not mind his being drunk, if you will let me come in; I am not afraid; he will not hurt me.'

'Well,' said the woman, 'you can come if you like; but he will only abuse you.' I said, 'Never mind that', and followed her up the stairs. I felt strong now in the Lord and in the power of his might, and as safe as a babe in the arms of its mother. I felt that I was in the path of obedience and I feared no evil. Oh, how much the Lord's people lose through disobedience to the leadings of the Holy Spirit! If they would only keep his words he would dwell with them, and then they need fear neither men nor devils.

The woman led me to a small room on the first floor, where I found a fine, intelligent man, about 40, sitting almost double in a chair, with a jug by his side out of which he had been drinking that which had reduced him beneath the level of the beasts that perish. I leaned on my Heavenly Guide for strength and wisdom, love and power, and he gave me all I needed. He silenced the demon, Strong Drink, and quickened the man's perceptions to receive my words. As I began to talk to him, with my heart full of sympathy, he gradually raised himself in his chair and listened with a surprised and half-vacant stare. I spoke to him of his present deplorable condition, of the folly and wickedness of his course, of the interests of his wife and children, until he was thoroughly waked up and aroused from the stupor in which I found him.

During this conversation his wife wept bitterly, and by fragments told me a little of their previous history. I found that she had once known the Lord, but had allowed herself to be dragged down by trouble, had cast away her confidence and fallen into sin. She told me that her husband had a brother in the Wesleyan ministry who had done all that a brother could do to save him; that they had buried a daughter two years before, who died triumphantly in the Lord, and besought her father with her dying breath to leave off drinking, and prepare to meet her in Heaven; that she had a son, then about 18, who she feared was going into a consumption; that her husband was a clever workman, and could earn three or four pounds per week as a journeyman, but he drank it nearly all, so that they were compelled to live in two rooms, and often went without necessary food. I read to him the parable of the prodigal son, while the tears ran down his face like rain. I then prayed with him as the Spirit gave me utterance and left, promising to call the next day with a temperance-pledge book, which he promised to sign.

I now felt that my work was done for that time. Exhausted in body, but happy in soul, I wended my way to the sanctuary, just in time for the conclusion of the service and to lend a helping hand in the prayer-meeting.

On the following day I visited this man again. He signed the pledge and listened attentively to all I said. Full of hope, I left him to find others similarly lost and fallen. From that time I commenced a systematic course of house-to-house visitation, devoting two evenings per week to the work. The Lord so blessed my efforts that in a few weeks I succeeded in getting 10 drunkards to abandon their soul-destroying habits and to meet me once a week for reading and expounding the Scriptures and prayer. We held three or four blessed little meetings, and I doubt not our numbers would have increased more and more, but, in the inscrutable workings of Divine Providence, my health gave way and I was most reluctantly compelled to abandon my happy and promising sphere of labour. I was shortly after removed from the town, and my way opened to a new and still more fruitful work in the vineyard.

You will not be surprised, dear reader, after this little sketch, to hear me say that I esteem this work of house-to-house visitation next in importance to the preaching of the gospel itself. Who can tell the amount of influence and power which might be brought to bear on the careless, godless inhabitants of our large towns and cities – nay, on our whole nation – if all real Christians would only do a little of this kind of work?

The masses of the people look upon Christians as a separate and secluded class, with whom they have no concern and possess nothing in common. They watch them go past their houses to their various places of worship with utter indifference or bitter contempt; and, alas! has there not been too much in our past conduct calculated to beget this kind of feeling, much of Pharisaic pride and selfish unconcern?

If the zeal of the Lord's house had eaten us up, if we had realised more fellowship with Christ in his sufferings, if we had understood the meaning of his words, 'Compel them to come in', if we had been baptised with Paul's spirit, when he could almost have wished himself accursed from Christ for his brethren's sakes, should we not have gone out amongst the people as our Master did, by the roadside and into their houses, to have spoken to them the 'words of this life', to have persuaded, implored, and compelled them to come in?

Alas, we are verily guilty – not, in many instances, for want of light or for want of the leadings of the Holy Spirit, but for want of obedience, and because of our pride or shame or fear.

Oh that, with all who read this, the time past might suffice to have walked after the flesh in this matter! Oh that from this hour you, my dear reader (if you are a child of God), would set yourself individually to this work. You can do it, however weak, timid or slow of speech. He says, 'I will be with thy mouth, and teach thee what thou shalt say' and 'It shall be given you in that same hour what ye shall speak.' All that is needful is for you to give yourself up to the leadings of the Spirit. Lean on him for all you want. He will inspire you with the constraining love, the melting sympathy, the holy zeal and the mighty faith alone necessary for the task.

This is the work that most needs doing of any work in the vineyard There are teeming thousands who never cross the threshold of church, chapel or mission-hall, to whom all connected with religion is as an old song, a byword, and a reproach. They need to be brought into contact with a living Christ in the characters and persons of his people. They want to see and handle the Word of Life in a living form. Christianity must come to them embodied in men and women, who are not ashamed to 'eat with publicans and sinners'; they must see it looking through their eyes, and speaking in loving accents through their tongues, sympathising with their sorrows, bearing their burdens, reproving their sins, instructing their ignorance, inspiring their hope and wooing them to the fountain opened for sin and uncleanness.

Dear reader, here is a sphere for you! You have long wished to do something for your 'blessed, blessed Master'. Here is work, boundless in extent, and momentous beyond an angel's power to conceive. For it, you need no human ordination, no long and tedious preparation, no high-flown language, no towering eloquence; all you want is the full baptism of the Spirit on your heart, the Bible in your hand, and humility and simplicity in your manner. Thus equipped, you will be mighty through God to the pulling down of strongholds. You will find your way to many a heart long since abandoned by hope and given up to despair, and in the great day of account you shall have many a sheaf as the result of your labour, and the reward of your self-denial.

I think I hear some timid one saying, 'Ah! I wish I could: the Lord knows how I long to be doing some real work for him; but I am so weak, and so little adapted to this kind of labour, I fear I should not succeed.'

My dear brother, sister, we are of little use in any department of the vineyard until we have been made to realise our own weakness. The weaker we feel ourselves to be, the better. It is not a question of our strength but of our faith. 'Why look ye so earnestly on us' (said Peter to those who marvelled at the miracle wrought on the lame), 'as though by our own power or holiness we had made this man to walk? ... Faith in the name of Jesus has made this man strong, whom ye see and know.'

God does not call us to any work in our own strength; he bids us go and do it in his. 'Give ye them to eat,' said he to the disciples, but he knew who must supply the bread. So now he requires us to break the Bread of Life to the multitude, trusting in him for the supply. He hath chosen the weak things of the world to confound the mighty. Why? That the excellency of the power may be seen to be of God, and not of man.

No matter how simple the words, or how tremulous the voice, if he blesses, then it shall be blessed. The 'Does you love God?' of a little child, accompanied by the 'demonstration of the Spirit and of power', will do more for Christ and souls than the most talented and eloquent sermon without it; for it is 'not by might nor by power, but by my Spirit, saith the Lord of Hosts.'

Dear reader, are you willing to be one of God's chosen ones? or will you anger him by saying, 'Send by whom thou wilt send' but not by me? Are you willing to trample on self, and, taking hold of the strength of omnipotence, to go in the power of his might, and do what you can? If so, his word to you is, 'Fear not; be strong, and of good courage; neither be thou dismayed: for the Lord thy God is with thee whithersoever thou goest' and 'Lo, I am with you alway, even to the end of the world.'

Six

Hot saints

Revelation 3:15: 'I would thou wert cold or hot.'

WHY does God like people to be hot in his service? For the same reasons that we like people to be hot in ours. We have no confidence in half-and-half, fast-and-loose friends; milk-warm adherents who in times of danger wait to see which way the wind blows before they commit themselves to our views or interests; servants who will serve us while at the same time they can serve themselves but the moment our interests and theirs appear to clash will leave us to our fate. We like thorough, whole-hearted, all-length friends and servants, and to such only do we confide our secrets or trust our important enterprises. We may use the half-hearted as far as they serve our purpose, but we have no confidence in them, no heart-fellowship with them, no joy over them. We would rather they were hot or cold out-and-out friends or foes.

Read in your own heart and mind, in this respect, a transcript of his and see the reason why he says: 'I would thou wert cold or hot.' I want you to note two or three characteristics of hot saints so that you may know whether you belong to the number.

To be hot implies the possession of light, purity, pungency, power.

Light: hot saints have such a halo round about them that they reveal and make manifest sins in others. They do this, first, by contrast. 'What fellowship hath light with darkness?'

The light of God flashed from a hot saint on the dark consciences of sinners makes them feel their sin, misery and danger, and if they will receive it, leads to their conversion. It 'opens their eyes' and if they will follow it, leads them to Jesus. 'Almost thou persuadest me to be a Christian ... Come, see a man which told me all things that ever I did ... Ye are the light of the world.' If sinners reject this light their rejection seals their sins upon them and renders their condemnation double. 'If I had not come and spoken unto them, they had not had sin; but now they have no cloak for their sin.' What a fearful responsibility rests on all sinners who are brought into contact with saints who are filled with the light of God. Some of you here are living under this light: How are you using it? Beware!

Secondly, light reveals sin by antipathy. 'Everyone that doeth evil hateth the light, neither cometh to the light, lest his deeds should be reproved.' The presence of a certain degree of spiritual light must produce either repentance or opposition. A dark soul cannot dwell in the presence of a soul full of light without either repenting or opposing. If it does not submit it will rebel.

It was under the hot blaze of this light that the Jews round about Stephen 'were cut to the heart, and gnashed upon him with their teeth'. The effect of his light on their darkness was to reveal their enmity and scorch them into a fury of opposition. When intense spiritual light and darkness are brought in contact, their innate antipathy makes them reveal each other. The devil could not endure the presence of Jesus without crying out, 'I know thee who thou art, the Holy One of God.'

How is it with you saints here in this respect? Can you get along with dark souls without eliciting their enmity? If so, depend upon it you have not much light; not that light which accompanies great heat. If you don't want to be spewed out of the mouth of God, see to it, that you get it!

Thirdly, light reveals sin by reproof. Hot saints will 'rebuke their neighbour and not suffer sin upon him'. They are full of zeal for the glory of God and jealousy for his honour; it breaks their hearts because men keep not his law. They know that they have the light of life, and they feel that they must hold it up over the wrongdoing, deception and hypocrisy of their fellow men in order to 'open their eyes and turn them from darkness to light'.

You never hear them apologising for sin or calling it by smooth names. They feel towards sin, in their measure, as God feels towards it. It is the abominable thing which they hate and therefore they cannot in any case allow it, pander to it or excuse it. Most saints will mercilessly turn the blazing lamp of God's truth on the conscience of a sinner with reproof as pungent, pointed and personal as Nathan gave to David, Jehu to Jehoshaphat, or Jesus to the Jews.

Purity: heat cleanses, purges away dross, destroys noxious vapours. So the burning fire of the Holy Ghost purifies the soul which is filled, permeated, with it, hence hot saints are pure. They purify themselves, as he is pure. Their garments are white, they keep themselves 'unspotted from the world'. They improve the moral atmosphere wherever they go. Their very presence reproves and holds in check the unfruitful works of darkness, and sinners feel as Peter felt when he said, 'Depart from me, for I am a sinful man, O Lord.'

Pungency: heat burns. Hot saints set on fire the hearts of other saints. They singe the consciences of sinners, burn the fingers of Pharisees, melt the hearts of backsliders and warm up those who have left their first love.

Power: hot saints are mighty. The Spirit is not given by measure unto them. They may not be very intellectual or learned, but their heat makes more impression on the hearts of sinners and stirs more opposition from hell than all the intellect and learning of a whole generation of lukewarm professors. The fishermen of Galilee produced more impression on the world in a few years than all the learning of the Jews had done in centuries because they were hot in the love and service of God.

Hot saints are more than a match for their enemies. Satan himself is afraid of them. 'Paul I know,' said he; yea, and he knows and fears all such. Wicked men cannot stand before them; the power of their testimony cuts them to the heart, and makes them either cry out, 'What must we do to be saved?' or, 'Away with him! Away with him!' Hot people are not only able to work, but to suffer. They can endure hardness, suffer reproach, contend with principalities and powers, fight with wild beasts, hail persecution and death!

To be hot ensures opposition – first from Pharisees. They look with contempt on hot people, call them fanatics, extreme people, troublers of Israel, disturbers of the peace of the Church, occasions of reproach to the respectable and reasonable part of the Church.

The Pharisees were the bitterest enemies of him who said, 'The zeal of thine house hath eaten me up.' And they are still the bitterest enemies of those who are filled with his Spirit. It matters not that they have now a Christian creed instead of a Jewish; the spirit is the same, and will not tolerate 'God manifest in the flesh'. A formal, ceremonious, respectable religion they do not object to; but a living, burning, enthusiastic Christianity is still Beelzebub to them.

Secondly, to be hot ensures opposition from the world. The world hates hot saints because they look with contempt on its pleasures, set at naught its maxims and customs, trample on its ambition and applause, ignore its rewards, abjure its spirit and live altogether above its level. 'Because ye are not of the world, therefore the world hateth you.' It can tolerate lukewarm religionists: rational, decent people who appreciate this world as well as the next and can see how to make the best of it, but these 'hot, pestilent, mad fools' who obtrude their religion everywhere, who are at everybody about their souls, who are always talking about God, death, judgment, heaven and hell: 'Away with them! They are not fit to live.'

Thirdly, to be hot ensures opposition from the devil. Oh, how he hates these hot saints! What trouble he takes to trip them! He knows they are worth it. Many a council is held in hell over these. They set fire to his standing corn. They rout his best trained legions. They shake the foundations of his throne. They take the prey out of his very jaws, they pull it out of his fires.

He must do something! He sets his principalities and powers to work on them. Loose and feeble fiends will do for lukewarm people, but these he must take in hand himself, and try all the guile and force of his gigantic intellect on them. He troubles them on every side, and, at last, when God permits, he has their heads off. He got Paul's, but they defy him even when they are between his teeth; he cannot swallow them. They escape out of his very jaws to glory, and who knows the mischief they work his kingdom, up there.

Hallelujah! Our arch enemy is a conquered foe. Let me remind you, in conclusion, that to be hot ensures God's special favour, protection and fellowship, and our final victory. 'Be thou faithful unto death, and I will give thee a crown of life.' Whereas to be lukewarm is to be spewed out of his mouth, which indicates special dislike, disgrace and final abandonment.

Which will you be: hot or lukewarm?

Seven

Conscience

Acts 24:16: 'And herein do I exercise myself, to have always a conscience void of offence toward God and toward men.'

PERHAPS there is no complaint more frequently on the lips of those who mourn over leanness of soul than this: 'My faith is so weak. I want more faith.' Doubtless a weak faith is the secret of a great deal of the barrenness and misery of many Christians but it never seems to occur to them to ask why their faith is weak, why they find themselves powerless to appropriate the promises of God. 'Yes,' said a dying backslider to a man of God who was trying to comfort him by quoting the promises, 'yes, I believe they are true, but somehow they won't stick!' The fault was in the state of his own heart. He could not appropriate the promises, because he knew that he was not the character to whom they were made.

Now it seems to me that a great deal of failure in faith is simply the result of a defiled conscience, and if those who find themselves weak and sickly in spiritual life would turn their attention to the condition of their consciences, they would soon discover the reason for all their failure. The fact is,

117

we have a great deal of so-called Christianity in these days which dispenses with conscience altogether. We sometimes meet with persons who tell us that they are not under the law, but under grace, and therefore they are not condemned, do what they will.

Now the question is, does the gospel contemplate such a state? Does it propose to depose or abjure conscience, or to purify and restore it to sovereign control? First, let us define conscience.

Conscience is that faculty of the soul which pronounces on the character of our actions (Romans 2:15). This faculty is a constituent part of our nature and is common to man everywhere and at all times. All men have a conscience; whether enlightened, or unenlightened, active or torpid, there it is; it cannot be destroyed. Therefore Christianity cannot propose to dispense with it, as God in no case proposes to destroy, but to sanctify, human nature.

There has been much philosophising as to the exact position of conscience in the soul: whether it be a separate faculty, as the will and the understanding, or whether it be a universal spiritual sense pervading and taking cognisance of all the faculties, as feeling in the body. It matters little which of these theories we accept, seeing that the vocation of conscience remains the same in both.

Second, let us glance at the office which conscience sustains to the soul. This office is to determine or pronounce upon the moral quality of our actions: to say whether this or that is good or bad. Conscience is an independent witness standing as it were between God and man; it is in man, but for God, and it cannot be bribed or silenced.

Someone has called it 'God's Spirit in man's soul', another 'God's vice-regent in the soul of man'. Certainly it is the most wonderful part of man. All other of our faculties can be subdued by our will, but this cannot; it stands erect, taking sides against ourselves whenever we transgress its fiat: something in us bearing witness against us when we offend its integrity.

Now it is a question of vital importance to our spiritual life whether the gospel is intended to deliver us from this reigning power of conscience and make us independent of its verdict, or whether it is intended to purify and enlighten conscience and to endow us with power to live in obedience to its voice.

Let us examine a few passages on this point. First, let us see what is done with conscience in regeneration. Hebrews 9:14: 'How much more shall the blood of Christ, who, through the eternal Spirit offered himself without spot to God, purge your conscience from dead works to serve the living God?' See also Hebrews 10:22.

Second, let us see the office which conscience sustains in regenerate men. 1 Timothy 1:19: 'Holding faith and a good conscience, which some, having put away, concerning faith have made shipwreck.' Romans 9:1: 'I say the truth in Christ; I

119

lie not; my conscience also bearing me witness in the Holy Ghost.' See 1 Timothy 3:9 and Acts 23:1. We have also set forth the consequences of allowing conscience to become defiled. 1 Timothy 4:2: 'Speaking lies in hypocrisy, having their conscience seared with a hot iron.' Also Titus 1:15.

There are many other texts quite as much to the point, but these are abundantly sufficient to show that Paul had no idea of a wild, lawless faith which ignored the tribunal of conscience and talked of liberty while leaving its possessor the bond-slave of his own lusts. The apostles clearly show that true Christianity no more dispenses with conscience than it does with the great moral law by which conscience is set, and to which it is amenable. Hence Paul tells us in our text that he exercised himself to have always a conscience void of offence.

Thirdly, we want to point out what is implied in having a conscience void of offence. This implies, first, a 'purged' conscience, made clean. Conscience must be made clean before it can be kept clean. The residuum of all sin settles on the conscience, and as all have sinned there can be no consciences clean by nature. There is only one way by which consciences can be purified, purged from guilt and made ready for new service: Hebrews 9:14: 'from dead works' from all pollution, uncleanness, sterility.

Conscience is not only polluted by sin but outraged, incensed, made angry. It needs to be pacified as well as purged and this can only be done by the blood of atonement. Every believer remembers the precious sense of purity and peace which spread over his soul when first he realised a saving interest in the blood of Christ. How sweet it was to feel that all the stains left by the sins of a past life were washed out; to realise that the anger and vengeance of an aggrieved conscience were appeased; that God, having accepted the Lamb as a sufficient atonement, conscience accepted him also, and was pacified!

The offence and condemnation of past sin is washed away and now the conscience is void of offence: clean and ready to serve the living God. There is a beautiful significance in the word 'living' in this connection. It seems to intimate that there is a fitness, an appropriateness, between the character of the Being to be served, and the quality of that faculty of the soul which has specially to preside over his service.

It is now not only made clean but light, quick, tender, ready to detect and reject everything old, rotten, impure, unholy, and to keep it out of the sanctuary of the believer's soul, as unfit for the service of the living God who sees every thought, motive and desire. And oh, how true is conscience to its trust, if only the soul would exercise itself always to obey!

The apostle laboured to have always a conscience void of offence. This must have been possible or he could not have exercised himself to maintain it. He was too good a philosopher for that. What unpardonable and wilful mistakes are made about Paul's experience! His personification of the ineffectual struggles of a convicted sinner in the words, 'Oh, wretched man that I am' have been wrested from their explanatory connection and set in solitary and mocking contradiction to every exposition of his experience from the hour of his conversion to that of his martyrdom.

Paul was either a sanctified man, 'more than conqueror ... doing all things through Christ strengthening him ... counting all things but "loss and dung" ... knowing nothing amongst men save Jesus Christ, and him crucified' or he was the greatest egotist that ever lived.

Neither was he honest, for we have not a word about failure or defeat after he once attained the liberty wherewith Christ Jesus made him free. And yet no apostle gives us so much of his personal experience as Paul. He continually exhorts the churches to follow his example, to walk as he walked, and tells Agrippa that he would both he and all that heard him were altogether such as he was, save his bonds.

He continually challenged his enemies to point out a single selfish or inconsistent action, declaring that whatever he did, or wherever he went, or whatever he suffered, it was all for the interests of his Redeemer's Kingdom. And when his work was done, like some mighty conqueror about to seize the crown of victory, he stretches forth his hand and cries: 'I am now ready to be offered, and the time of my departure is at hand. I have fought a good fight; I have finished my course; I have kept the faith.'

Surely Paul had found it possible to maintain a conscience void of offence! And so may we. But this implies, secondly, systematic obedience to the dictates of conscience. Being made pure, light and quick, and set on the throne of the soul to communicate the light and truth of God, and to witness impartially whether it is obeyed or not, of course there can be but one way to keep this conscience void of offence, and that is by so acting as not to offend, grieve or incense it again!

You see, if the soul – nay, the whole being – refuses to be in subjection to it; will not obey it; then conscience must needs take offence again, because it cannot be cheated, or bribed or silenced. To be kept void of offence it must be obeyed with promptness. To parley is to defile. How many a soul has dated its ruin to temporising with a suggestion which conscience asserted ought to have been put down at once!

Thirdly, to keep a conscience void of offence requires unremitting effort, exertion, 'exercise', determination; a bringing up, so to speak, of all the other powers and faculties of the being. 'Herein do I exercise myself' – the whole man, soul, mind, body; myself.

Here is need for 'exercise' indeed. This signifies no child's play; no mere effervescing emotion, expending itself in sentimental songs or idle speculations. Here is 'the fight of faith', the faith of the saints, which can dare, and do, and suffer anything rather than defile its garments Only those who thus fight have the apostle's kind of faith.

Satan knows this and he waylays such souls with every temptation possible to them. He tries considerations of ease, interest, honour, reputation, friends, fashion, health, life! And sometimes puts all these in one scale at the same time, over against a pure conscience in the other. Alas! How many, for such considerations, 'have put away a good conscience, and concerning faith have made shipwreck'?

It is no uncommon thing to meet with people in this condition, who, 'having built again the things they once destroyed, have made themselves transgressors'. Conscience is defiled and incensed, and demands that the evil shall be put away and repented of, and the soul cast afresh on the blood of atonement for pardon and healing. Instead of doing this, however, we are constantly meeting with people who try to cling on to what they call faith, and who quibble and reason to try to make it out that they are right; but between their sentences we fancy we can hear their consciences mutter, 'You know you are wrong, you know you are guilty; confess, and forsake your sin.'

I know a young lady, a professing Christian, who was deeply convinced by the Spirit of God that the business in which she was engaged was inconsistent with her profession, and also with her becoming a real follower of Jesus. After much controversy she took three days to debate with conscience as to whether she should give it up or not. Minister, friends, everybody but conscience, said, 'No'. She yielded, and 'put away a good conscience' in order to keep a good business. Shortly after, she married a young man with the same sort of religion as her own. They rushed into imprudent and extravagant expenditure; he soon failed, and now she is in seas of trouble and sorrow. Surely 'Thine own wickedness shall correct thee, and thy backslidings shall reprove thee.'

Fourthly, to keep a conscience void of offence requires the subjection of the whole being to the will. As conscience is the reigning power of the soul, the will is the executive, and in order to keep a pure conscience the will must act out its teaching. When inclination lures, when the flesh incites to that which conscience condemns, the will must say, 'No!' and be firm as adamant, counting all things but dung and dross.

When Satan takes us up to the pinnacle and says, 'All these things will I give thee' if thou wilt do this or that, the will must say, 'No!' and repel the tempter. This is just the point where human nature has failed from the beginning. Our first parents fell here. Their consciences were on the right side, but their wills yielded to the persuasions of the enemy. This is sin: the committal of the will to unlawful self-gratification. Joseph's conscience thundered the right path, and his will acted it out. Pilate's conscience also thundered the right course, but his will failed to carry it out. In one we behold a hero, in the other a traitor!

Young man, when you have got the fiat of your conscience, act on it. At all costs carry it out. Better be counted a fool, and die poor, than be damned as a traitor to God and righteousness!

Young woman, what says your own conscience about accepting that unconverted lover? I entreat you, obey! Never mind what friends say; what inclination says; what apparent interest says. They all lie, if they contradict God! And miserable comforters will they all prove when his chastisements overtake you. Let your will be firm, though it slay you.

Man of business, conscience intrudes even on the arena of trade. You hear its voice about this and that practice, or such and such a scheme. Does your will carry out its dictates? Do you resolutely say, I will not 'do this thing and sin against God'? This is the test of faith. Real faith dares trust God with consequences; a spurious faith must look after consequences itself! It must save its life whatever becomes of a good conscience. Judge ye how much it is worth!

Fifthly, to keep a pure conscience requires great vigilance, lest by surprise or inattention we defile it. 'What I say unto you, I say unto all: watch.' Our enemy is always watching to put an occasion of stumbling in our way. He knows the power of surprise. He lays many a snare to take us unawares; many a nicely-laid plot; many carefully-adjusted circumstances to catch us by guile. Oh, what need for vigilance! If by subtlety we ever get overcome, what must we do? Lie down in guilt and despair? Allow conscience to remain polluted and incensed? No! Up and confess, and forsake, and wash again.

Sixthly, to keep a pure conscience requires patience. It often necessitates our walking in an isolated path, taking a course which men condemn. Men judge from outward appearance, they do not see the intricacies of individual experience. The very course which they condemn may be that which conscience insists on, and which must be done or suffered, or conscience and God be grieved and offended.

Patience will wait till God, by time and providence, justifies our course. Paul said it was a small matter with him to be judged of man's judgment. Why? Because his conscience acquitted, justified, and God witnessed that he was right. Such a soul can go on with all the world up in arms against it. This is just what the martyrs did: nothing more, nothing less.

Lastly. A pure conscience is its own reward. No matter who condemns, if it approves, there is peace and sunshine in the soul. And whatever our trials or persecutions, we can draw near to God without wavering, for 'If our heart condemn us not, then we have confidence toward God. And whatsoever we ask, we receive of him, because we keep his commandments, and do those things that are pleasing in his sight' (1 John 3:21, 22).

As a clean conscience is its own reward, so an offended conscience is its own punishment. Conscience frequently offended soon becomes 'seared' – mark, not destroyed; quick and raw enough underneath, ready to be probed and fretted by the worm that dieth not and scorched by the fire that never goes out but seared on the surface, of no use for present service; numbed, dark, useless.

People with their consciences in this state often tell us they do not feel condemned for dispositions and practices which are evidently forbidden by the Word of God, nor for things which they once would have trembled to do. Poor things, they do not see that their consciences are seared.

A lady once told us that early in her religious experience she would have felt very much condemned if she had gone to a theatre, but now she could go there and feel that she was sitting with Christ in Heavenly places at the same time! She had got such an increase of light, or rather darkness, that the godless entertainment, the worldly multitude, the flippant jokes and pot-house songs did not strike her as inconsistent with the teaching and profession of him who said: 'They are not of the world, even as I am not of the world.'

Truly, it is an awful thing to have a seared conscience! There is but one step between that soul and everlasting death. Is there one of this class here? My friend, make haste back to the foot of the cross, confessing and forsaking your sins, and get your 'conscience purged (again) from dead works to serve the living God'. For 'without holiness no man shall see the Lord'.

Eight

Aggression

Mark 16:15: 'Go ye into all the world, and preach the gospel to every creature.'

ACTS 26:16-18: 'Rise, and stand upon thy feet: for I have appeared unto thee for this purpose, to make thee a minister and a witness ... unto whom now I send thee, to open their eyes, and to turn them from darkness to light, and from the power of Satan unto God, that they may receive forgiveness of sins, and inheritance among them which are sanctified by faith that is in me.'

I want you to note that the great idea in both these texts is that of determined aggression on the territory of Satan. 'Go ye into all the world, and preach the gospel to every creature.' What a commission! Who has ever yet grasped all that it implies? The vast obligations imposed on the people of God in this command have never yet been more than half realised. Go ye – not build temples or churches and wait for them to come to you, but go ye, run after them, seek them out, and preach his gospel to every creature.

Thrust yourselves and your message on the attention of men. The commission to Paul, and through him to us, embodies the same idea: 'Unto whom now I send thee, to open their eyes.' They are indifferent, preoccupied, asleep in their sin and danger. 'I send thee as my herald' to arouse them, shake them, open their eyes, make them think and realise the verities of eternal things! We are to do this as God's ambassadors, whether men like it or not. We are not to wait for convenient seasons, but in this most urgent business to be instant 'out of season'. We are not to shrink from pressing the truth on men's attention for fear of giving offence. He who gave the commission has foreseen and provided for this result. 'I will appear unto thee; delivering thee from the people, and from the Gentiles, unto whom now I send thee' (verses 16, 17).

Secondly, it is implied in both these commissions that this aggression will provoke opposition. Of course it will. Who ever heard of aggression on the territory of an enemy without opposition, according to the power possessed by that enemy? Such a thing is impossible naturally, and even more so spiritually. 'The whole world lieth in (the arms of) the wicked one ... The strong man armed keepeth his goods.' And if we, armed by a stronger power than he, take them, we must expect opposition.

Our Lord systematically taught his disciples to expect and prepare for persecution. He taught them that their principles, motives and objects would be so incomprehensible to men of a worldly spirit, whether Pharisees or worldlings, that they would inevitably persecute and oppose them. Such we find was the case wherever the gospel was introduced. Magistrates, rulers and mobs set themselves in array against both the preachers and their truths. I take it as one of the worst signs of the Christianity of this age that it provokes so little opposition, for it is as true now as it ever was, that if we are not of the world, the world will hate us, and he that is born after the flesh will persecute him who is born after the Spirit.

Thirdly, I want you to note that the only law laid down in the New Testament for the prosecution of this aggressive warfare is the law of adaptation. 'I am made all things to all men, that I might by all means save some' (1 Corinthians 9:22). 'And of some have compassion, making a difference; and others save with fear, pulling them out of the fire' (Jude, verses 22 and 23).

The gospel message is laid down with unerring accuracy, in unalterable terms. We are not at liberty to change even the order of it as given from the glorified lips of our risen Lord to Paul. 'To open their eyes, and turn them from darkness to light, from the power of Satan unto God, that they may receive forgiveness of sins and inheritance among them that are sanctified by faith that is in me.' Here is the Divine order: first, conviction; second, repentance; third, forgiveness; and woe be to the man who transposes this order. He makes as great a mistake as one would make in putting the key into the lock upside down. He who made man laid down this order, and it fits our mental and spiritual constitution. Let us take care to preserve it intact.

Let us keep the message itself unadulterated and the order of it undisturbed; but in our modes of bringing it to bear on men we are left free as the air and sunlight. Adaptation, expediency, is our only law. I may convey it in any kind of language so that it carries the true meaning to the mind of the hearer. Words are nothing, only as they convey ideas.

I may send it through any kind of agent, from the acute and polished intellect of a profound theologian down to the newborn babe in Christ, scarcely able to read a letter in the Book. Any man, however common or unclean he may have been, if God hath cleansed him, may be used to open the eyes of his fellow-men and turn them from darkness to light.

Adaptation is the great thing we ought to consider. If one method or agent fails, we should try another. God does so. How he tries by various methods and strokes of providence to bring men to himself! In how many ways did he strive with you, my brother, my sister? He did not try one providence, one sermon, one consideration, one call, but oh, how many, with some of us, before our stubborn hearts yielded to his grace!

And as he works, so he calls us to work with him. In this sense: to become all things to all men, if by any means we may save some; of some making a difference, pulling them out of the fire. That is, adapt ourselves and our measures to the social and spiritual condition of those whom we seek to benefit.

It is here I conceive that our churches have fallen into such grievous mistakes with reference to the propagation of the gospel in our own times. We have stood to our stereotyped forms, refusing to come down from the routine of our forefathers, although this routine has ceased to be attractive to the people – nay, in many instances, the very thing that drives them away.

The most thoughtful writers on education tell us that the first essential in a teacher of youth is to be able to interest his pupils. True. This is equally true of the people. If you would benefit and bless them, you must interest them. You must clothe the truth in such garb, and convey it by such mediums, as will arouse their attention and interest their minds. In short, we must come down to them. Whatever has caused it, it is a fact that the masses of the people have come to associate ideas of stiffness, formality and uninteresting routine with our church and chapel worship, and if we are to be co-workers with God for them, we must move out of our jog-trot paces and become all things to them in order to win them.

If they will not come inside our consecrated buildings, we must get at them in unconsecrated ones, or out under the canopy of Heaven. And has not Jesus by his blood consecrated every spot of earth to soul-saving purposes? If they will not listen to our college-trained and polished divines, we must send them men of their own stamp, whose habits of thought and modes of expression are familiar and congenial to them, and who – washed and filled with the Holy Ghost – are as well adapted to preach to them as were the fishermen of Galilee to the men of their generation.

Why did not our Lord fit and call the divines of his own times to go to the people? He certainly could have done so! Surely he must have had a sound and philosophical reason for choosing fishermen. He acted on the principle of adaptation. Instead of working a miracle to unteach and set loose the divines for this work, he acted on existing natural law, as he always did when there was no necessity to break it, and chose the best adapted instruments for his purpose. Hence he chose men from amongst the people to be workers together with himself, and sent them out into the byways and hedges, the fields, the market-place, the seashore and the hillside. In short, he sent them wherever the people were to be got at. Oh! if the Church had steadily adhered to the tactics of our Lord, who can tell whether the kingdoms of this world would not long since have been subjected to his sway?

For our part, at any rate, we cannot hesitate for a moment as to the conduct demanded of us by the teachings of our Master, and of experience, as well as by the exigencies of a perishing world. We would a thousand times rather err in too readily utilising men and means that are manifestly suitable to the accomplishment of the great end in view, than in rejecting any man or any means as 'common' or 'improper' which may aid us in the gigantic labours which a dying world stands in such terrible need of.

Nine

The uses of trial

*James 5:11: 'Ye have heard of the patience of Job,
and have seen the end of the Lord; that the Lord is
very pitiful, and of tender mercy.'*

AFFLICTION occupies a large place in the
economy of salvation, for though suffering is the
result of sin, God takes hold of it and transmutes it
into one of the richest blessings to his own people.
From whatever secondary causes the afflictions of
the righteous may arise – whether from the sins of
their forefathers, the cruelty of their enemies, their
own mistakes, or the mistakes of their friends, or the
malice of Satan – it is their blessed privilege to realise
that the Lord permits and overrules all, and that he
has a gracious end in every sorrow which he allows
to overtake them. Happy the Christian who, though
he cannot see this 'end' at present, is able to trust in
the goodness which chastens, and cleaves to the
hand that smites.

It may help us, however, to 'endure chastening' if
we consider two or three of the gracious ends, or
uses, of our trials.

Firstly, trial reveals us to God. There is a sense,
doubtless, in which trial reveals us to God; makes

manifest to him what is in our heart. Perhaps someone may object and say, 'No, no; we need nothing to make manifest to God what we are. He understands us perfectly. He knows what is in man, and needs not anything to tell him.' True! And yet he says of Abraham: 'Now I know that thou fearest God, seeing that thou hast not withheld thy son, thine only son, from me.' And to the Israelites: 'And thou shalt remember all the way which the Lord thy God led thee these forty years in the wilderness, to humble thee and to prove thee, to know what was in thine heart, whether thou wouldst keep my commandments or no.'

Now God knew that Abraham feared him, and he also knew how far Israel would keep his commandments, but he did not know as a matter of actual fact until the fact transpired. He must have the latent principle developed in action before he could know it as action. Thus Abraham by his obedience to the painful command made his love manifest to God. Not that God had previously any doubts of Abraham's love, but he desired a practical manifestation of it towards himself, or to know it in action.

The divine love is like all other love in this respect, it delights in practical proof of love in return, nor will it be satisfied without. Remember this, Christian, in thy various afflictions. The Lord is leading thee about in the wilderness to prove thee, and to see (to make manifest to himself) what is in thy heart, and whether thou wilt keep his commandments or no.

Remember also that in nothing is love made so manifest as in willing, cheerful suffering for the sake of its object. It is easy – nay, joyful – to labour, but patient, cheerful suffering requires a deeper love, a more perfect self-abandonment. 'Greater love hath no man than this, that a man lay down his life for his friends … We glory in tribulations also.'

Secondly, trial also reveals us to ourselves. Although we do not agree with the adage that untried grace is no grace at all, yet unquestionably much fancied grace has proved itself, in the hour of trial, to be but as the early cloud and the morning dew. 'How many who have received the Word with joy and for a while have believed, in time of temptation have fallen away.'

How many a professing Christian, if he could have had predicted to him the effect of adversity upon his heart and life, would have said with Hazael: 'Is thy servant a dog that he should do this?' And yet when the true test of character was applied he fell. When he had eaten and was full, then his heart rebelled, or when he was chastened by the Lord he grew weary and said, 'Verily I have cleansed my heart in vain, and washed my hands in innocency.'

There is no surer test for the Christian as to the state of his heart than the way in which he receives affliction. How often, when all has appeared prosperous and peaceful, and the child of God has been congratulating himself on spiritual growth and increased power over inward corruption, has some fiery trial overtaken him, which, instead of being met with perfect submission and cheerful acquiescence, has produced sudden confusion, dismay and perhaps rebellion, revealing to him that his heart was far from that state of divine conformity which he had hoped and supposed.

Thus the Christian often suffers more from a consciousness of insubordination under affliction than from the affliction itself. Dear reader, how is it with you in this respect? When trials overtake you, are you able to say, 'It is the Lord, let him do what seemeth him good' and 'I know that thou in faithfulness hast afflicted me'? Are you able to realise that 'whom the Lord loveth, he chasteneth' and that these light afflictions are working a future increase of glory?

If so, happy are you. This is the best of all evidence to yourself that the divine Spirit is working in you to will and to do of your Father's good pleasure. This fruit does not grow on the corrupt soil of unregenerate nature; it springs only from a heart renewed by the Holy Ghost and baptised into fellowship with Christ in his sufferings.

But is it otherwise with you? Does your heart chafe, and fret and rebel? Are you saying, 'All these things are against me'? If so, this is proof that the work of grace is at a low ebb in your soul, that your faith is weak and your spiritual perceptions dim. It is high time for you to awake out of sleep and cry mightily unto God for a revival of his work in your heart and for a sanctified use of the affliction which has overtaken you.

If God dries up the water on the lake, it is to lead you to the unfailing fountain. If he blights the ground, it is to drive you to the tree of life. If he sends the cross, it is to brighten the crown. Nothing is so hard as our heart, and as they lay copper in aquafortis before they begin to engrave it, so the Lord usually prepares us by the searching, softening discipline of affliction for making a deep-lasting impression upon our hearts. The fire our graces shall refine, till, moulded from above, we bear the character divine, the stamp of perfect love.

Thirdly, trial also reveals us to the world. As the greatest manifestation of God to the world was by suffering, so the most influential revelation of his people to the world has been by suffering. They are seen to the best advantage in the furnace. The blood of martyrs has ever been the seed of the Church. The patience, meekness, firmness and happiness of God's people in circumstances of suffering, persecution and death have paved the way for the gospel in almost all lands and all ages. A baptism of blood has prepared the hard and sterile soil of humanity for the good seed of the Kingdom, and made it doubly fruitful.

The exhibition of the meek and loving spirit of Christianity under suffering has doubtless won thousands of hearts to its divine Author, and tamed and awed many a savage persecutor, besides Saul of Tarsus. When men see their fellow-men enduring with patience and meekness what they know would fill themselves with hatred, anger and revenge, they naturally conclude that there must be a different spirit in them. When they see Christians suffering the loss of all things and cheerfully resigning themselves to bonds, imprisonment and death, they cannot help feeling that they have sources of strength and springs of consolation all unknown to themselves.

Patient suffering, cheerful acquiescence in affliction and anguish – mental or physical – is the most convincing proof of the divine in man which it is possible for humanity to give. 'Truly this was the Son of God,' said those who stood by the cross when they saw how he suffered. And how many who have been thoroughly sceptical as to the professions of their converted kindred, and have most bitterly persecuted them, and withstood every argument and entreaty advanced in health and activity, have yielded almost without a word before the patience and peace with which the billows of suffering and death have been braved – nay, welcomed! Such evidence is too mighty, such proof too positive to be resisted, even by persecutors and blasphemers.

Abraham might have written a book and preached all his life long, as doubtless he did, but the whole, ten times told, would not have convinced his family, his contemporaries and posterity of the depth and fervency of his love to God, as did that holy calm surrender of the best beloved of his soul to the requirements of God.

Job might have been the upright, benevolent, righteous man he was, but probably we should never have heard of him but for his wonderful submission, patience and faith under suffering. It is this which lifts him up as an example and a teacher to all succeeding generations. It was when sitting on the dunghill, apparently forsaken of God and man, and suffering the direst physical agony which Satan could inflict, that Job attained his greatest victory and made that wonderful exhibition of trust in God which has been the comfort and admiration of God's people from that day to this.

It was in the fiery furnace that Shadrach, Meshach and Abednego won such glory to the God of Israel that even a heathen king proclaimed his majesty and dominion, and commanded his subjects to worship him who could deliver after this manner.

It was in the furnace of persecution that Stephen, Peter, James, John and Paul proved the divinity of their characters and the genuineness of their faith. Without suffering, the world could never have known the strength of their faith, the fervency of their love or the purity of their lives. Their trials made them 'spectacles unto the world, to angels and to men' and won for their Master the ears and hearts of thousands.

When an apostle would present to us the mightiest achievements of faith and the most wonderful exhibitions of the power of divine grace, he refers us not so much to the doings of God's people as to their cheerful and triumphant sufferings (Hebrews 11).

Dear reader, how are your afflictions revealing you to those around you? Are you adding your testimony to that of the cloud of witnesses who are gone before, to the sufficiency of divine grace to sustain and comfort in the hour of sorrow and suffering? Is your patient endurance saying to those who are watching you, I can do (and suffer) all things through Christ which strengtheneth me?

Watched by the world's malignant eye,
Who load us with reproach and shame;
As servants of the Lord Most High,
As zealous for his glorious name,
We ought in all his paths to move
With holy fear and humble love.

That wisdom, Lord, on us bestow,
From every evil to depart;
To stop the mouths of every foe,
While, upright both in life and heart.
The proofs of godly love we give,
And show them how the Christians live.

Ten

Prevailing prayer

I fear there are comparatively few Christians who know what prevailing prayer is, because they do not comply with the conditions on which alone it can be offered. I regard these conditions as threefold:

First, living and abiding union with Jesus. 'If ye abide in me, and my words abide in you, ye shall ask what ye will, and it shall be done unto you' (John 15:7).

Second, systematic obedience to the teaching of the Word and of the Spirit. 'Beloved, if our heart condemn us not, then have we confidence toward God. And whatsoever we ask, we receive of him, because we keep his commandments, and do those things that are pleasing in his sight' (1 John 3:21, 22).

Third, unwavering faith in the veracity and faithfulness of God. 'But let him ask in faith, nothing wavering. For he that wavereth is like a wave of the sea driven with the wind and tossed. For let not that man think that he shall receive any thing of the Lord' (James 1:6, 7).

Of course there are many other passages of similar bearing and of equal weight but I regard these three as clearly setting forth the conditions of prevailing prayer, constituting, as it were, the three steps of successful approach to the mercy seat. They are like three links of a golden chain connecting our souls with God, and if one be missing or defective, the power to prevail in prayer is lost.

Does not this explain the reason why there is so much ineffectual prayer in our day? Christians get hold of a promise, and try to work themselves up to faith for its fulfilment, but, alas! one of the conditions is wanting, one of the links is broken. Their own hearts condemn them: 'Then have they (no) confidence toward God, and whatsoever they ask they receive (not) of him, because they keep (not) his commandments, and do (not) those things that are pleasing in his sight.' How can a man approach God in confidence, when he is living in the daily practice of something for which his own heart condemns him? Impossible! As soon might Satan offer effectual prayer. Before that man can truly approach to God, he must 'cleanse his hands … purify his heart … and put away his iniquity'.

No matter what our creed or opinion, God has made it a law of our spiritual being that without submission and obedience there can be no confidence. Faith in Jesus is God's expedient for bringing us back to obedience, and not for saving us in disobedience. And all the way through the New Testament he refuses to accept any other proof of discipleship than that of obedience.

No less than six times in the 14th and 15th chapters of John is this criterion insisted on. 'Faith without works (obedience) is dead' and therefore has no power to take hold of God or to appropriate his promises. I am satisfied that this is the 'missing link' in the experience of multitudes of professors, and in vain do they cry, 'Lord, Lord' while they do not the things that he says. In vain do they try to assure their hearts before him while they love not in deed, but only in word and in tongue.

I am afraid there is much Antinomianism abroad, which makes Christ the minister of sin and which is always crying, 'Faith! Faith! Only believe!' while consecration and obedience, as indispensable accompaniments of faith, are entirely lost sight of.

'How can ye believe,' said our Lord to some in his day, 'while ye receive honour one of another, and seek not the honour that cometh from God only?' And we may say to some in our day: how can ye believe who prefer self-indulgence, wealth or worldly conformity, to Christ and his cross and the extension of his Kingdom?

Is it not still true that 'if any man love the world, the love of the Father is not in him' and that 'the friendship of the world is enmity towards God'? Saving faith in the sinner and prevailing faith in the believer are alike impossible without full consecration to known duty. If any one disputes this, let him try to exercise faith in any given promise or for any given blessing while he is refusing obedience to the claims of God or withholding part of the price which God requires, and he will find, whatever may be his preconceived notions on the subject, that it is simply impossible.

Herein is the solution of the question so often asked: 'How is it that there are so few answers to prayer?' David affirmed it when he said, 'If I regard iniquity in my heart, the Lord will not hear me.' Neither will God hear and answer us, call we ever so loudly and ever so long, if we willingly consent to any known unrighteousness.

How fares it with your prayers, dear reader? Do you know that God hears you by the answers he vouchsafes? If not, may not this be the reason for the miscarriage? God is unchanged and unchangeable, the promise faileth not: 'All things whatsoever ye shall ask in prayer, believing, ye shall receive.' God must be true, and if your experience contradicts the sure word of promise, you may be certain that it is your experience which is at fault.

Examine yourself. Repent and do your first works. He is faithful and just to forgive the sins of his people and to cleanse them from all unrighteousness. And then bring all the tithes of a wholehearted, loving and believing service into his storehouse and prove him therewith, and see if he will not open you the windows of Heaven and pour you out such a blessing that there shall not be room enough to receive it.